Uncomplicate It

HOSANNA WONG

Uncomplicate It

Permission to Enjoy God in Your Unique Way

W Publishing Group

An Imprint of Thomas Nelson

Uncomplicate It

Published by W Publishing, an imprint of Thomas Nelson, 501 Nelson Place, Nashville, TN 37214, USA.

The author is represented by Illuminate Literary Agency, www.illluminateliterary.com.

Thomas Nelson titles may be purchased in bulk for educational, business, fundraising, or sales promotional use. For information, please email SpecialMarkets@ThomasNelson.com.

ISBN 978-1-4003-4758-2 (softcover)
ISBN 978-1-4003-4761-2 (ePub)
ISBN 978-1-4003-4762-9 (audiobook)

HarperCollins Publishers, Macken House, 39/40 Mayor Street Upper, Dublin 1, D01 C9W8, Ireland (https://www.harpercollins.com)

Library of Congress Control Number: 2025942754

Art Direction: Meg Schmidt
Cover Design: Lindy Kasler
Interior Design: Denise Froehlich

Printed in the United States of America

25 26 27 28 29 LBC 5 4 3 2 1

To the over one thousand people who vulnerably shared your stories with me and the personal and unique ways that you enjoy God. You have transformed my life and uncomplicated how I see life with God for forever*. Thank you. Here's to a thousand conversations and* counting . . .

Contents

Part 1

This Is Your Permission Slip

CHAPTER 1

Am I for Real?

"I am a fake."

I will never forget when he said it. The doors of the bus had closed beside us, and the rumblings of its engine faded away as we stood there staring at each other. Bustling street sounds surrounded us—cars honking, kids being let out of school—and yet it all seemed like muffled white noise in the background of that Twilight Zone moment of my childhood. I felt frozen. We both began to well up with tears.

In this moment, I am in high school. I am wearing a Superman t-shirt, and my hair is twisted in two side buns like Princess Leia, because clearly, I am the epitome of fashion and cool.

Just kidding. I was not cool. And yet this boy liked me. I was on top of the world believing he would even consider a girl like me. I thought he was the coolest. I thought he, his family, and his church were everything I wanted to be.

He came from a family of pastors and said he would one day be a pastor too. He sang and played guitar on the church worship team—I loved that part of the service! All his brothers and sisters played some sort of instrument, sang, spoke, or led at his church. His parents were leaders in multiple outreaches and well known in the community. And they seemed to know God in ways I had never imagined. They expressed their worship to God in ways I had never seen before. They had a faith that seemed unshakable. They had a depth I longed to have. They held prayer events for hours into the night. They were spiritual athletes—gold-medal Olympians in the games of godliness.

I wanted to *be* them.

It wasn't a secret that they did not approve of us dating. I did not come from a family with a background like theirs, and they would remind me of it. My dad had battled addiction for over fifteen years. After he came to know God, every part of his interior and exterior life changed. He started an outdoor outreach to our friends who were living without homes and battling addiction, and that is where he would raise us kids.

I loved our friends and the family we made on the streets, and today, I am so thankful for how I was raised. But back then, I knew my family was different from other families, and certainly our "church" was different from other churches. The simple story of a God who loves, redeems, and restores . . . *beautiful*. But spending two or three days a week outside—amid brick buildings wrapped in graffiti and trimmed with trails of trash and torn-apart tents, the scorching hot San Francisco city cement, and people bringing their beer, dirty needles, and multiple girlfriends to listen to the message? Maybe not everyone's perfect picture of church. *I get it*. But I wanted this boy's family to feel like I could learn to be more like *them*. Specifically, I wanted to impress his parents. I so badly wanted them to accept me. And I wanted them to teach me everything I needed to know.

When they'd ask me why I didn't do certain things in

worship, I would say that I wanted to and asked if they could explain it to me.

When they'd ask me questions about the Bible, I'd feel like I was failing at a critical quiz and would say that I didn't know, but wanted to know, and asked how I could learn.

I had questions. I needed things explained. I wanted to know more than the simple stories of God I learned on the streets at my outdoor church; I wanted to know the complex stuff. I wanted to know the *real* church stuff. I wanted to know God as much as they knew God. I wanted to experience God in *their way*, which I believed was the *right* way. And also . . . I *really* wanted to date this guy.

But I struggled with not feeling good enough. Not good enough to date this boy. Not good enough to be accepted by his family, his group of friends, or his church. And I did all I could to try to earn a status of faith that would deem me worthy.

Which is why I was so surprised when his fingers started to unwind from mine, when he pulled his hand back and said he needed to end things between us. He said he had no choice. His family did not approve. It's not like we were serious or even officially dating. But my high school self (in all my glorious fashion trends) was tender and deeply disappointed.

Standing at that bus stop, I managed to ask shakily, "Why am I not good enough? I'm doing all I can. What can I do better? I'm going to all the events. I'm reading all the devotions. I'm doing all the things you and your family are telling me to do. *What more can I do?*"

He started tearing up. I had never seen this side of him before.

And then he said it.

"I am a fake."

He may have said more words that I missed in my utter

blanking out, but when I mentally came to, small puddles of my tears had already formed shapes on the sidewalk.

"None of this is real to me," he continued. "I am faking all of it. I don't know who I am. I don't even believe any of this. I don't feel close to God. I don't know if anyone actually does. I'm just doing what I think I'm supposed to do. I'm just doing what other people do. I just know how to pretend. I am just faking it."

The bus that had left our corner was now swallowed in a puff of exhaust. It moved on, hopefully to pick up people in the distance who knew where they were going. Unlike the two of us.

That was a line-in-the-sand moment for me.

I had never—*ever*—imagined that some people might be faking a relationship with God.

I had never conceived of the possibility that some people might just be going through the motions they were taught in church but not actually experiencing anything real.

And here I was, feeling *not enough* for not doing what other people were doing. I was seeing how other people experienced God, and worshiped God, yet I felt like I was on the outside looking in. I felt moronic every time I asked questions about things I didn't understand and was left feeling less-than for even asking.

And now the truth was revealed.

For some people, it wasn't real at all. Some were putting on a spiritual show.

To be fair to this boy, we were both still in high school. (I hope he's somewhere out in the world, doing well and totally crushing it.) And to be fair to his family and his church, I have no idea about their personal relationships with God, and I did not feel like he was speaking on behalf of everyone. Just himself.

But the impact of that conversation was great. Though I was crushed by my crush, that was no longer my greatest concern. As he walked away and the next bus arrived, I stepped into that capsule of strangers—and as I made my way to the back, my mind was running like a treadmill on high speed. As the bus headed to my side of the city (more rough around the edges and miles from where he lived), I looked out the dirty window and asked myself these questions: *How can I tell if some people are real or fake? How do I know if they really know God? How can I be sure that it's real for them?*

But by the time the bus reached my side of town, my thoughts had arrived somewhere else as well. Somewhere more vulnerable. Somewhere far more personal.

My question became: *How can I be sure this is real for me?*

This One Thing

I have spent years of my life trying to answer that one question—which has led to a long line of many more questions waiting to be answered.

How can I know God for real . . . *without any ounce of faking it?*

How can I stop feeling so overwhelmed by all these unrealistic expectations? How can I stop feeling like I'm always letting God, myself, and everyone else down?

How can I enjoy God *and* enjoy my life?

How can I make sure I don't miss out on the life God has for me?

Is it possible for my time with Him to feel less like an obligation and more like a joy?

How can I stop comparing my relationship with God to other people's relationships with God?

Is there really only *one right way* to experience God?

What if that *one right way* doesn't work for me?

Why does something so critical have to feel *so complicated*?

My guess is that if you're holding this book, you have similar questions.

And here is the freeing truth:

Your relationship with God does not have to look like anyone else's relationship with God.

Exhale.

What?

It's true.

I wish I had known that sooner.

I wish I'd never compared my connection to God to anyone else's connection to God. I wish I hadn't spent years of my life thinking that I had to spend time with God in the exact same way I saw other people spending time with Him. Or that the way I talked to Him, worshiped Him, or enjoyed Him had to look one precise and pristine way . . . *or else.*

Your relationship with God does not have to look like anyone else's relationship with God.

I wish I had known earlier that the freedom, the peace, and the joy I was searching for would not come through looking like a specific kind of Christian or achieving a certain status in the church or in my life. But that it would come only through a true connection to God Himself. The Creator-of-the-universe-who-loved-us-so-much-He-sent-His-one-and-only-Son-Jesus-to-die-for-us God. I wish I'd known how very possible it was to have a real connection with Him and that that connection could be deeply personal. That it would be specific to me and God. And that it would involve my unique personality and quirks—which He intentionally created—plus my chaotic neighborhood, complex relationships, and colorful life that He'd placed me in.

Maybe then I would not have lived weighed down by some kind of "super Christian" expectation, overwhelmed by the churchy things I felt I had to do or feeling guilty about all the ways that I was convinced I was constantly missing the mark.

That is why I have written this book.

I want you to know this: Your relationship with God? You can uncomplicate it.

This message is for anyone who has ever felt like they want to know God for real but are unsure of how to do so in real life, right now.

In your current season of life, in your real job, and with your demanding schedule. With your needy family. With your exhausting coworkers. With *your* personality, the way *you* learn, the things *you* enjoy, and the things you *don't* . . . Is there a way for *all* of us to know God? Or is that reserved for the spiritual elite? Only the extremely disciplined? Only those with prim and proper lives and perfect routines? Only those who are morning people and embody the perfect balance of extroversion and introversion? Only those with family schedules that are perfectly in sync, who never have calendar conflicts . . . *not even once in a while*?

Is that what this must take?

What about those of us who cannot add one more thing to the to-do list?

What about those of us who can't start one more thing we feel like we're going to fail at?

What about those of us who are juggling so many family and work responsibilities that there doesn't ever seem to be time for a minute with God?

What about the rest of us who know how to put on a show

and pretend like we are close to God, but we are in a season of our lives where we want no part of that? We are over putting on a façade. We have no desire to pretend.

What about those of us who want real peace, real purpose, and actual joy in our real lives?

There's a way for all of us too.

This book is for anyone who has ever felt like they don't fit the mold they once thought they had to. (Spoiler: Some of the things we were taught may have been wrong.)

This is for anyone who has ever felt not churchy enough for their churched friends and too churchy for their unchurched friends (same).

This is for anyone who has seen movements of God and witnessed gatherings of His people but has felt like none of it seems real or relatable. As a result, maybe you don't want any part of it. Or, if it was real for *them*, and *that's* what it looked like to be real with God, then it couldn't possibly be right for you. *No way*, you're thinking. *No way could* that *be what it looks like to be real with God. And if it* was *real for them, then it couldn't possibly be right for me.*

I wrote this book with three people in mind:

First, the *curious*. You have just put your faith in Jesus. (That is the best decision you could ever make, and I would love to be your guide to help you truly know Him in a personal way!) Perhaps you want to know where to begin. You want your next steps to be clear and doable. This is for you.

Second, the *cautious*. You once felt connected to God, but you no longer do. You're not sure where to start or how to restart. You're not sure if it's possible to ever be the old version of you. (It's not, and that's a good thing!) You're not sure how you feel about God's people. You're not sure if you want to look like or live like the other people you know who follow God. You want to experience the God who created the universe, but you're not sure how that will work with your personality or lifestyle. This is for you.

Third, the *committed*. You are someone who has known God most of your life, but it has been hard to find purpose or peace in your current season. Perhaps you believe that Jesus is alive but you don't feel like your own soul is. You have felt your heart grow hard and cynical. You have started feeling uncharacteristically bitter toward other people. Perhaps you feel exhausted from trying to meet other people's expectations, or perhaps you're the most exhausted just trying to meet your own—the way you thought your life *should* look at your age, the community you thought you *should* have, the faith you thought you *should* have, the perfect routines you thought you *should* follow. Why does everyone else seem to be doing this just fine, but you're not? You have moments of feeling defeated. You sometimes feel like your life is on hold and you are waiting for a more ideal season to feel truly connected and filled. You know God, but you are not in a place of enjoying Him or enjoying your life.

As it turns out, many of the expectations we put on ourselves do not come from God. And so you can safely release them—drop them right where you are.

That is the freedom we will unpack in these pages.

That is the holy uncomplicating I will guide you through.

This is not a book with more to-do lists. In fact, you will find some to-don't lists. You will find some things you absolutely no longer should do.

Many of the expectations we put on ourselves do not come from God.

So much of what I thought it took to have a relationship with God was wrapped up in opinions and teachings from people who were either wired to experience God in totally different ways from me or were straight-up misrepresenting God, His character, and what it would take to know Him. I have spent most of my life trying to unpack what God *actually* says about how to know Him, enjoy Him, and live the way I've been created to live—and that's what I want to share with you.

If you and I were sitting together at a bus stop; standing in line for smoothies, coffee, or boba; or walking around a neighborhood park, and you told me you wanted to experience God for real in your real life, I wouldn't tell you whose faith yours should look like or which motions to go through to fake it. Instead, I would hand you the rest of these pages and say, "This is your permission slip. You can be who you are. You can embrace the season you're currently in. And that is the way to fully receive what God actually has for you."

Because I have *actually* discovered how this can be real for *me*. Throughout these pages, you will discover how this can be real for *you*.

CHAPTER 2

What If I Don't Fit in a Box?

What does the so-called perfect follower of Jesus look like?

What personality traits come to mind? Kind, humble, and hopeful? Somber and subdued? Positive and perky with a pearly-white smile stretching from ear to ear? Is there a specific style of clothing that comes to mind? Formal, casual, brand-new clothes, or thrifted, sustainable, perhaps hand-sewn? Do they carry out a certain set of routines, attend particular events, listen to specific music, or reshare certain posts on social media?

Do you have someone in mind?

You may despise the kind of person you are thinking of, or you may admire them so much you hope to be just like them. Growing up, I was the latter. I so badly wanted to follow God the best that I could and to do all the things a perfect follower of His would do.

I would look at the experts, authors, and influencers teaching on all the holy habits and assume that any way they engaged with God was the gold standard. I believed I needed to match them perfectly. *If I just worship like her, read my Bible like him, and pray without ceasing like them, then I will have the ultimate connection with God!* I thought there was a box I had to fit in, a level I needed to unlock, a person I had to look like. But a question I couldn't ignore nagged at me: *What if I don't fit in their box?*

What if my personality is different from that of the person I look up to? What if the ways I rest are different from those of the leaders I listened to? What if I have a different learning style? What if I have different tastes in music, fashion, and things I find fun? What if the pace of my life is far different from hers? What if my schedule looks nothing like his? Is giving my life to God about giving up everything I like and everything I enjoy and everything that makes me . . . *me?*

Absolutely not.

Yes, God wants to help you get rid of anything that stands in the way of a relationship with Him. And we'll talk more about that later. (Spoiler: Those things don't make us more of who we really are.) But sometimes we think God wants us to change *everything* about ourselves in order to have a relationship with Him. And that could not be further from the truth.

The truth might surprise you. Let this sink in:

God created you.

God hand-made your details.

God loves your details.

God thought all your details were important in order to know Him, love Him, love others, and live a full, purposeful life.

God did not invite you to be in a relationship with Him and then ask you to abandon all the details of the personality He created you with.

What if your details are, in fact, a key part of how God knew you would connect best with Him and best with others?

Do you want a real relationship with God? Do you want to fully enjoy your life?

God loves your details.

Great news: You already have what it takes. You've been set up for success.

Your personality is a part of how God wants to connect with you. Your personal tastes are a part of how God wants you to connect with others. The ways you feel rested and find peace? The ways you have fun? The ways you feel moved, inspired, and motivated? God created those ways in you. God created your interests with your best interests in mind.

How would it change our lives to see our personalities, schedules, and passions not as roadblocks but as pathways to enjoying God? How would it change your posture to know that you are already set up for success to connect with God?

Say this out loud to yourself right now: "I am set up for success."

Now quieter and slower for your soul to process it:

"I am set up for success."

It's almost as if the Creator of the universe wanted to know you and created you with that very goal in mind. And 100 percent—that's what He did.

Steer into the Skid

I was a California girl who had never once driven in snow. All my experiences in snow up to the point of meeting Guy—my then-boyfriend and now-husband—had been in the back seat of a car going up paved mountains to ski lifts and other safe, controlled environments. All to say, my nerves were shaky the first time he drove me around his hometown of Grand Rapids, Michigan, after fresh snow had fallen late at night.

As we drove from dinner to his parents' house, I noticed how some cars slid a bit at the stop signs. I grew worried. I all but screamed when one car coming down a hill couldn't stop at the intersection—and even though every other car had the right of way, they anticipated what was happening, stayed put, and accommodated the rogue car. It skidded in a circle in the middle of the intersection but quickly recovered and continued down the road, while traffic around it proceeded to move slowly and smoothly. No accidents, shouts, or hand gestures came from the other drivers.

Guy saw my stunned face and said, "We're used to snow here. We all know how to make space for each other, go with the flow of traffic, and keep each other safe." I was amazed at the room that was made and the grace that was given to that driver. (We Californians might not be known as the *most* chill drivers ever. Just saying.)

Then I asked, "How did that car that slid not crash? How did they know what to do and recover so quickly?"

"They steered into the skid," he said, then began explaining something that was very normal to him but brand-new to me. He said that, when in a panic mode, sometimes people will try to veer the opposite way of where the car is sliding because it might feel like the best thing to do—but the truth is, you want to veer *into* the skid. This means turning your steering wheel toward the side where your rear wheels are sliding. "Go in the natural direction the car is going. That's what's best for you, your car, and the flow of traffic. That's best for safety and power."

This analogy has stayed with me. So often when I go through hard or confusing times or need direction from God, I assume I need to engage with Him in a way that is opposite from my natural tendencies. The truth? I can steer into the skid. I *should* steer into the skid. I can veer into the natural movement of how I was created. Not only is that better for me and for the people around me, but I am not exerting energy trying to go against how I was created. Instead, I am going to unlock the best way for me to be close to God.

We might be surprised that we can steer into the skid of how we are wired, to truly encounter God. This is best for us and everyone around us.

Are you an introvert or an extrovert? Good.

Are you a late-night person or an early-morning person? Great.

Do you find peace in the outdoors or at home reading a book? Or both? Wonderful.

Do you process best in community and conversation or being alone with your thoughts? Perfect.

I will ask you more of these sorts of questions throughout the book, but I want to tell you up front: However you are made, that is on purpose. I want you to see your natural tendencies as good things. I want to help you unlock the parts of your personality that are actually pathways to encountering God. I want you to steer into the skid.

Are you an introvert or an extrovert? Good.

Looking to other people to see how they encounter God can be a beautiful thing. It can encourage you, inspire you, and show you new ways you may want to try yourself. But when our being inspired turns into rigidly trying to copy and paste their lives and become just like them, it goes from being helpful to hurtful. Teaching people a one-size-fits-all approach to connecting with God is the perfect way to create a culture of faking it.

But from the beginning of this book, we've declared that's

not what we want. We want real relationships with God. How will you find that? By being who you really are and interacting with God in your real life—with your actual schedule, with your quirky personality, and with the unique things you are wired to enjoy.

The Favorite Kids

My family is a basketball family. My dad used to sing a silly, sweet song about how he and my mom met on a basketball court. Both of my parents loved to play and raised all of us kids to love it too. We listened to Golden State Warriors games on the radio and shot hoops at local parks, and my brother and I went on to play in inner-city leagues growing up.

To this day, we all love basketball. (Steph Curry, if you're reading this, we love you.)

When I was eighteen years old, my dad passed away. When he died, my sister was twenty-seven, and my little brother was twelve. The grief was different for each of us, and so was the healing. The memories we replay are also different. Why? Because our relationships were different. We had different perspectives, different personalities, and different things that brought each of us closer to our dad.

I know my dad is not here to defend himself, but I am going to shoot my shot and go on record to guess that all three of us were his favorite.

My sister was his first kid. She had a special place in his heart. She was his favorite to play music with. They both played guitar, and she also played piano, and they would sing in our living room or sing loudly on the streets of our outdoor church, worshiping God together. My sister was from my dad's previous marriage, and he didn't even meet my mom until my sister was seven. She and my dad had a special bond because of those years—they had overcome a lot together. And as they worshiped and declared the faithfulness of God together, their connection was filled with so much history and so much power.

My brother was my dad's only son. He had a special place in my dad's heart. My dad would cheer loudly as my brother played tee-ball growing up, jumping up and down and screaming obnoxiously as my brother ran the bases. Of course, my brother would soon learn basketball, the family sport. He was my dad's favorite to throw balls to, whether teaching him how to hit them with a bat or shoot them in a basket. He was the kid living at home when my dad passed away, and he'd been the one who helped my mom take care of my dad in his final days. They will always have a special bond because of that.

I'm my dad's middle child. I had a special place in his heart. Though he was known to many as a powerful man of God, my friends and I knew him as the funniest guy in the room. I think I was his favorite to make jokes with. I understood his humor. We would give each other glances across a busy room and know exactly what the other was thinking. And no matter what errands or house chores we were doing, we were constantly making jokes, singing songs, and playing games, often crying laughing at ourselves. Through financial hard times, losses, and eventually my dad's death from cancer, I can't say we had the easiest life. But we always found a way to have some happy in the middle of it. We had our own special bond too.

So how can *you* have a real relationship with God, your loving Father?

I promise you this: It won't look exactly like mine does. And that is a good thing.

This is not a book about how to have a one-size-fits-all relationship with God.

God wants a personal, authentic, one-on-one relationship with you. This relationship will be different from your siblings', your spouse's, your friends', or that one person's on social media. And that's good! God is not "putting up" with your personality or "giving you grace" for what brings you true joy. No, this is His perfect plan. This is what God thought would be fun for you and for Him.

Why would God create us differently if He ultimately wanted us all to connect with Him in the exact same way?

Why would God create us differently if He ultimately wanted us all to connect with Him in the exact same way?

As it turns out, He doesn't want us to be the same. He wants real relationships with each of His kids.

One Thousand Favorite Kids

I have been on a journey the past few years of unlocking the various ways that people experience God. That journey is why you're holding this book today. Through sixteen years of traveling and teaching at churches, prisons, outreach events, conferences, and conventions around the world, I have found that no one person who has a real and vibrant relationship with God has the exact same one as someone else.

Why?

Because one person is a single mom with three kids.

One person is a college athlete with practice six days a week.

One married couple has endured job changes for what seems like forever, so their schedules are always changing. One woman just lost her husband to cancer and feels like she is starting over in every area of her life. One college student just lost both parents in an accident and is now taking care of her two younger siblings.

One recording artist is touring around the country, and his schedule feels out of control and without routines he used to have. One couple just sent their youngest off to college, and at the dawn of their empty-nesting era, they are learning who they are and how to connect with God, and each other, again.

The answer is not for all of us to fit into one glorious God-box. The answer is not for all of us to have the same schedule and life plan, nor is it to live weighed down by guilt and shame over not having the schedule we once did. Not at all. The answer is to embrace the lives we have right now—to embark on journeys of engaging with God in our real lives.

What would it look like for *you* to enjoy God and enjoy your life with its real, everyday schedule?

To help you unpack this, I did something a little zany.

I asked over a thousand people from around the world about their experiences connecting with God. I asked them these two questions:

1. What has stood in the way of you connecting with God?
2. What *is* a unique way you have found to connect with God?

Do you know what I discovered? Over one thousand different answers from over one thousand different people. People with different schedules, different backgrounds, and different personalities.

It was incredibly emotional conducting these interviews, feeling like I was being let in on personal and profound secrets. It was heartbreaking at times to replay the audio recordings of our conversations. I would often tear up on my big blue couch relistening to some of the roadblocks that stood between people and God, the expectations and shame, and the ways we have greatly overcomplicated it. It was also exhilarating and encouraging beyond my wildest dreams to hear the ways people said they had bulldozed through roadblocks and discovered fun and unique ways to encounter God. Some of these ways I had never thought of before!

Throughout this book, I'm going to be sharing these findings with you. I am convinced they will encourage you just like they encouraged me, especially if you have ever felt like

- you don't have as much time as you'd like to connect with God
- you're not sure if you're doing it right
- you have far too much to do already
- you don't want to fail at one more thing
- you can't figure out how to connect with God the way other people do
- you're not connecting with God the way you used to
- you're not a morning person
- you can't focus
- you have a busy life
- you're too far from God
- you're not worthy

You are not alone. I want to name the roadblocks that have held us back. I want to introduce doable shortcuts to encounter God even in the midst of your unique season and schedule. And for the record, all of these ways come with flexibility, grace, and permission to pivot.

I pray that as you turn the pages of this book you will feel lighter, not heavier. I pray that these conversations free you, that some make you laugh, and that they inspire you to have your own conversations with people as well, to keep digging up ways we can all encounter God. I pray these one thousand conversations are not merely the end of a journey but instead the beginning of a thousand conversations and counting between you, me, the people in our lives, and people all over the world. I'm praying for a Great Uncomplicating—that we all discover how simple connecting with God can be. That we all unlock how we've been wonderfully wired to enjoy Him. I pray you steer into the skid of who you are and that you discover a unique, one-on-one relationship with a loving God . . . perhaps even stealing delightful insider glances at each other across a busy room that nobody notices but the two of you.

CHAPTER 3

What Am I Made Of?

"The family is picking us up."

We were standing on a dusty road surrounded by hills wrapped in lush vineyards like emerald gift-wrapping paper. The bus that had brought us to this remote corner of Tuscany could no longer continue where the narrow dirt road was going. A small family winery was our destination, and since they didn't cater to mass tourism, their driveway wasn't wide enough for a bus—so my husband, Guy, was letting me know they were coming to pick us up in compact cars to drive us up their road.

We had taken a trip to Italy with a group of friends, and this was the part of our trip I was looking forward to the most. By then, I had studied vineyards, vines, and branches for seven years. I had even taught and written on them. But there were still so many questions I had burning within me . . . questions I was one winding road away from getting answers to.

This is where my fascination had started. Jesus' students (disciples, apprentices) had many questions about how to live well, and one of the answers Jesus gave them was this:

"Abide in Me, and I will abide in you."[1]

He continued, "A branch cannot bear fruit if it is disconnected from the vine, and neither will you if you are not connected to Me. I am the vine, and you are the branches. If you abide in Me and I in you, you will bear great fruit. Without Me, you will accomplish nothing."[2]

Enter: a fascination with vineyards.

I love the idea of connecting to Jesus and flourishing in my life. That is the kind of life I long for. But the truth is, for most of my life when I read those verses or heard them in church, they sounded beautiful and spiritual but also hypothetical. There weren't many vineyards on the streets I grew up on. I couldn't fully grasp this picture. And I couldn't figure out *how*: How do I abide, what does abiding even look like, and how would that play out in my actual life?

I've been unpacking the answer for years. Guy will tell you: Unpacking its goodness has truly changed my everyday life. I thought I had unearthed all there was to discover . . . until this one eye-opening trip to Tuscany.

So, please kindly consider this book an update to my previous teachings on abiding. As I discovered, there was much more to be mined. Like Beyoncé once said, *I want to upgrade you.*[3] Like when you go to a Mexican restaurant and you expect chips and salsa, but then the staff brings you chips and salsa . . . and queso? That's an upgrade! I want to add some queso to my previous understanding of abiding in Christ.

Where Do I Start?

Niccolò (because of course his name was Niccolò) picked up Guy and me and drove us along winding hills with canopies of branches and blooming flower buds enveloping us. There was something very regal about it all, as if we were being brought through a magical forest to an enchanted castle, except that it was all very humble and unassuming. Our tiny car rocked back and forth, bumping along the rocky driveway before pulling into the family's sacred space.

This was no fairytale castle. This was a home built from scratch, with three distinct vineyards on the property that the family had planted, tended, and nurtured for many years. Their business was rooted in a strong belief in family, relationships, and stewardship of all that the vineyards produced—not just wine but also food items, soaps, creams, and paint.

After years of studying how to "abide," with my nose pressed into the pages of books and staring at vintage photographs (with occasional visits to a supercool lab—more on that to come), I was ready to see my research come to life and to experience it in 3D. I was also ready for some of my findings to perhaps be challenged, since I would be learning from actual boots-on-the-ground winegrowers (*vignaioli* in Italian), standing on their home soil in the heart of their vineyards. I was hoping that this family that had lived and breathed vineyards would awaken in me far more than scientific and agricultural books could ever teach me.

Boy, did they ever.

As we walked past their home, following along the winding road that led to a wide-open field, Niccolò pointed to three vineyards surrounding us. He explained that the owner of the winery, Annibale, had planted three distinct vineyards on different parts of his hilly land and named each after one of his three beloved daughters. Each vineyard had its own unique type of soil, environmental factors, and weather quirks, just like his three girls each had their own interests, temperaments, and personalities. It was the differences in each vineyard that brought out unique qualities in their grapes and created the richly varied flavors in their individual wines.

Although Niccolò wasn't a blood relative, he said Annibale, Annibale's wife, and Annibale's daughters were like his second family, so he could describe each daughter in detail. As the resident agronomist—aka crop scientist, aka wizard of wine, as I liked to call him—he was also able to meticulously describe the unique qualities of each vineyard.

As we headed toward the vineyard named after the youngest daughter, I asked Niccolò, "What if I wanted to start a vineyard?"

He laughed and exclaimed, "You do?"

I know this is not a picture book, so you can't see me in this moment; but nothing about me gives off a deep-in-the-dirt-farmer kind of vibe.

After all our hearty laughter had died down, I said, "No, I don't! But *what if* someone came up to you and said they truly did want to start their own vineyard and grow the best grapes? What is the first thing you would tell them? What advice would you give?"

I thought this might bring some inspiring insight into how we as Christ followers could begin our own journeys in flourishing. Perhaps his advice could help those of us who want to begin connecting with *the* Vine. Perhaps he could give me the top ten best steps to growing perfectly. *That would be killer!* I thought to myself. *I could write a book about it! Ten chapters, ten steps. Instant holy and happy life!*

That's not how it played out.

He thought about it. The crunch of gravel beneath our feet was the only sound between us as we approached the youngest daughter's vineyard, along with a few passing birds chirping above us. Finally, he stopped walking. He looked up at me. And his answer surprised me.

"I don't first have any advice for you," he said. "First, I have questions."

From the Hills to Our Homes

"What kind of soil do you have?"

It wasn't the groundbreaking spiritual advice I was hoping for. But it certainly was a grounding question.

"Every soil is different," he continued. "All over the world you'll find very different soils. Even in the area we are in, the vineyards down the road and the ones a few miles farther away all share similar weather patterns and resources—but our soil is different. Even our own three small vineyards have different soil. You must ask yourself: What are you working with? What are you starting from? If you want to start growing, I will first ask about your soil."

I was speechless. I could tell Guy was too. My mind was going a million places and I was having trouble forming a follow-up question.

As if he read my flooding mind, he continued in his broken English, "The second question I have is: What's your idea? What's your hope?" He pondered for a bit. "What's the word I'm trying to say?"

Guy offered, "Dream? Vision?"

"Yes!" he replied. "The vision you have for what you want. Maybe it's a certain grape. Maybe it's a certain wine you want to make. Maybe it's a certain business or lifestyle. Or maybe you are like *our* vineyard. Our idea, our vision, was building a community that creates and produces many different things for many other families to come and enjoy. One big enjoying family. So that was *our* vision. What's the vision *you* have?"

As he started walking again, we followed and eventually

made it to the other side of that vineyard. As we looked out over the ravishing rows of grapes, I remembered to ask, "What other questions would you have for me?"

He shook his head. "Those are my only two questions. Because your soil and your vision will dramatically change your next steps. There is no next step that works for every soil and every vision. So first, know those two things, then you make a plan."

Unfazed by the finality in his words, I continued to shoot off a bunch more questions I had written down in my quest to nail down all the perfect next steps to the secret of abiding I had hoped for. *Certainly, he could give me something more specific!* I had to know the right way.

He graciously responded to my fire-hydrant flooding of questions. "You know, I have been working in vineyards quite a while. And I have to say that with all your questions and all that comes with biology, science, agriculture, and everything I know that is related to growing in life, the most truthful answer I can give to you is—it depends." And he shrugged and opened his arms in a full-bodied Italian gesture, as if to underline his meaning.

Then, at the top of the new vineyard we were approaching—the one named after the owner's middle daughter—he spread his arms even wider to signal its vastness and said, "I mean!"

Niccolò smiled back at us, arms spread wide, as if to say, "Look at the beauty of this one."

We did.

We stood in awe of how different but equally beautiful this vineyard was.

Finally, he turned back to Guy and me and said, "Like I said, it all depends. This vineyard is similar to the last one, and so close, too, so you might think it's exactly the same. Except look at its position toward the sun. There's less natural shade. Also this one is on much flatter ground. That brings different challenges. The next one we are going to is much rockier than this. But far more shade. So also different benefits and different difficulties. All to say, we have different systems for growing on this one than for the last one, and more different systems for the next one I'll show you too. So just know that it depends.

"There's no specific next step written exactly for every living organism with every soil and every vision in every season. There are different roadblocks from the changing environments, weather, and limitations, but there are also different advantages. We have many different ways of accomplishing what we set out to do. But you must know where you're starting and where you want to go. Then we go from there."

With that, we started walking along the vineyard named after the eldest daughter, a field with different shading and a different position to the sun than the last. This one was uniquely beautiful as well.

Your Vineyard

When it comes to flourishing in your one and only beautiful life and growing in your own unique faith, it can be easy to compare yourself to others. You may look across at the voluptuous vineyards and thriving journeys of faith of a sister or brother or parent or friend or person on social media, become awestruck by what you see, and think, *That's amazing. How did they get there?*

Like me (as demonstrated by my questions to Niccolò), you might also assume there's a surefire how-to guide that provides the next perfect steps to get where your role models are. *The Foolproof Guide to Flourishing.* Or *Perfect Spiritual Growth for*

Dummies. But as Niccolò pointed out, the answer is not one-size-fits-all. It really boils down to two simple questions.

What Kind of Soil Do You Have?

What are you made of? We might think of soil or dirt as . . . well, *dirty*. Fair enough. But this question is about more than the messy mud you're starting with. It's also asking, What are the nutrients within it, what are the other things we can learn from its composition? For example: Where do you come from? What moments in your past have shaped who you are? What has shaped your ideas of yourself, of God, or of God's church?

For me personally, I was raised by parents who really loved Jesus. And I was *also* around *other* people who were good at quoting Jesus but not living like Jesus. And because of that, as I shared in the first chapter, my past shaped a perspective that not everyone's faith is real—but mine can be. That's how I approach God. An advantage I have is that I have seen others demonstrate how to love Jesus for real. However, I have also seen fake versions of following Jesus—and it's been difficult at times to tell the two apart.

That's my past and my perspective. Because of this, I come to Him *without* the illusion that faith always needs to look a certain way. I come to Him *with* the knowledge that some people have misused and misrepresented Him. I come with a tender and desperate desire not to look like the people around me but for my experience with Him and conversations with Him to be honest and personal. That's *my* soil.

Ask yourself: *How has my past shaped my perspective of God and of my life?*

It's important you know what you are made of. Otherwise you'll try to grow a relationship with God the same way someone else does but without their unique kind of soil. The best way to flourish? Know your own soil. Know what you're made of.

And acknowledge what season you're in *now*. What is currently weighing on your heart?

Know your own soil. Know what you're made of.

Perhaps someone you love is very sick, and you are begging God for them to live a longer and fuller life than what you've been told to expect. Perhaps someone you love has recently passed, and you're angry at God and want help, peace, and comfort. Perhaps you are stressed about finances, and you need wisdom from God and doors to open. Perhaps you are unsure about your next step for your career and you need direction. Perhaps you are raising kids all alone and you are praying for a partner. Perhaps you recently welcomed a newborn in your house and you really need a nap.

Ask yourself: *What do I need from God in this season?*

As I sit in my soil writing this to you—with my background, my past, and my present—I know where I am from and what my greatest longings are today. Now it's your turn.

What Is Your Vision?

What do you want your life to produce? What do you want your relationship with God and others to look like? Beyond your past and present pains, what is your hope for the future? What are your hopes for your relationships? What do you hope a healthy church community or friend group could look like? We might all hope for the same general things: happiness, health, and comfort in our homes. Those are wonderful things. Pray for those things. But some of us may have never articulated to God or to anyone else some of the greatest, most specific desires of our heart.

Maybe it's to be a loving parent. Maybe it's to have a home

with an open door that's a safe and welcoming place for many. Perhaps it's to find a church community where you feel no guilt or shame, you love the people there, and you love encountering God with those people. Maybe it's seeing your friends more. Maybe it's being a beacon of encouragement on social media. Maybe it's helping your work environment be a more positive place. I don't know what it is for you. But those desires are specific. They say something about you. They say something about the way you've been wired. Steer into the skid.

If you don't name those desires or ever express them to God or other people, you may miss out on important ingredients of who you are. *It's good to have holy expectation*—to know what you dream of and also to pray to God for it. Your life may not look exactly how you thought it would. But the desires God has given you were not made to stay dormant. They were made to be nurtured. They were made to be the ground where good things grow.

What is your soil, and what is your vision?

Once you answer these two questions, we can better map out a pathway for you to flourish.

And for the record, what God wants for you? What God's vision is for your life? It's a full, enjoyable, faith-filled life through connection with Him.

In John's gospel, Jesus said, "The thief comes only in order to steal and kill and destroy. I came that they may have *and* enjoy life, and have it in abundance (to the full, till it overflows)."[4]

To enjoy God *and enjoy your life* is one of God's purposes for you. It's His vision for you. And with your soil in mind, He has made a way for you to grab hold of it.

This is what I will help guide you through as we walk the soil of your unique vineyard, map out your unique vision, and break through the roadblocks in the way. When you identify where you are starting and where you hope to go, you will be better equipped to live the life you truly desire to live. And it might not look like other people's lives. In fact, it probably shouldn't. The weather may be different in the season you're in. The soil may be different where you are. There are people who did not come from where you've come from. You may not be made of the same things others are, and perhaps they could not imagine being made of what you're made of. The specifics of your vision may be different as well. As we unpack a thousand conversations with a thousand different people with a thousand different soils, we will discover that there is no one-size-fits-all advice here. There are not ten strict steps for every person ever to flawlessly accomplish this. But there *is* a way for all of us to uniquely grow and flourish.

To enjoy God *and enjoy your life* is one of God's purposes for you.

How?

Well, it depends . . .

CHAPTER 4

Roadblocks and Shortcuts

I am the last person you want to recruit for your trivia team.

Though my husband, family, friends, and I are all big fans of board games, card games, and friendly and fun competitions (sometimes), the one night I know I will be picked last in the draft is trivia night. Quirky questions and deep-cut references to pop culture, movies, and music in the seventies, eighties, and nineties might sound like your dream night. For me, it's the opposite. Here, I have a roadblock.

I did not grow up with a television.

My family did not have a TV in our house my whole childhood, except for about a two-year stretch when my mom was pregnant with my little brother, Elijah, and a bit after he was born, and we borrowed a friend's TV that only played VHS tapes. Sometimes, when we moved its antennae just right, we also got one channel that played cartoons on Saturday mornings, and I would sit with baby Elijah and watch *Justice League* with so much glee, so excited to have a TV at all! Other than that, we watched one of the few VHS tapes my mom had of whatever rom-coms were big in 1995 and 1996. I may or may not have seen Sandra Bullock's *While You Were Sleeping* over fifty times.

For this reason, there's a lot of pop culture I have missed. Guy calls them my "gaps." We'll be out to dinner with friends, and they'll be referencing a popular movie or song from our childhood, and everyone will be in on the generational joke when Guy will say, "Hosanna has no idea what you're talking about. It's one of her gaps!" My friends will hurry to catch me up as quickly as possible, pulling out their phones for all the research and visual references I might need. The dinner inevitably turns into an epic classroom of pop-culture history.

This is no exaggeration. I have so many pop culture gaps. There are almost two decades' worth of time that I still have a lot to catch up on.

In school growing up, I felt very aware of this roadblock. I didn't know the songs the kids were singing, I didn't know the shows they were talking about, and I didn't know the celebrities they looked up to. On the streets where we had outdoor church and I learned the art of spoken-word poetry, I would hear the music my friends played on the radio, but it was mostly eighties and nineties hip-hop. So to this day, I know very little of the Backstreet Boys' deep cuts but a lot of Biggie Smalls and Tupac. That's simply how I was raised.

I remember feeling embarrassed as a kid, left out of conversations, and whenever friends were getting tickets to see bands I had never heard of, it was really hard to convince my dad to let me go. Because of the unique way I was raised, I have this one unavoidable roadblock.

Perhaps you feel like you have some too. Now, you probably

know much more about the music and movies that were popular when you were growing up. But maybe you feel you have some gaps when it comes to knowing things about God. Gaps when it comes to knowing certain things about faith, church, or what certain scriptures mean. Gaps when it comes to having a relationship with God, how it can be real, and what that even looks like. Gaps when it comes to giving yourself grace and receiving God's grace when you feel you're not living up to your own expectations.

I don't want you to grow frustrated. I don't want you to feel defeated. You may have been raised in a different environment from other people, and like me, you may have some roadblocks.

What, then, can we do? Are we just stuck in the dark forever? Are some people just super-spiritual, and we aren't? Are some people biblically savvy, and we aren't? Are some people more set up to be close to God, and we aren't? Do some people just have the right temperaments to be close to God, and we don't? Is everyone going to play God trivia without us?

I used to think my "gaps" meant something was wrong with me. Then when I married my husband, I started to see them in a totally different way. He didn't see them as roadblocks, something to be annoyed by or something that stood in the way of us having lively conversations or going to certain concerts. He saw them as *opportunities*. He got to show me all those movies I had missed. He got to take me on a journey through decades of comedy, sci-fi, mystery, and romance. He had a whole list of experiences he wanted to have with me.

He showed me the movie *Ferris Bueller's Day Off*. I had never heard of it. He found a podcast that recapped it, and we listened to it together. We discussed it over wings and fries and laughed our heads off. Every joke was new to me.

He showed me *Titanic*. I wept and I wept. I could not fall

asleep because I had so many questions and was going through so many emotions. I told Guy, "We have to tell people about this movie! Everyone needs to see it!" He put his arms around me, and in the most gracious and hushed tone, he whispered, "My love, everyone else *has* seen it."

We have been married for over eleven years, and to this day, there is still so much on his list he wants to experience with me. Why?

Because what I saw as a roadblock, Guy saw as an opportunity. What I saw as something that stood in the way of us connecting, he saw as a shortcut to connection, a way to bond with me—first his friend and later his wife—in a way he'd never been able to connect with anyone else before. Now every movie and band from a certain era I get to experience *with* him, through his lens, and with a lot of fun, laughs, and yes, late nights on Google surfing fan theories because I *still can't believe Jack dies in the end!*

Sorry if I spoiled the movie for you. If you've never seen it, you have some gaps, and you should probably take care of that.

For some of us, this isn't too different from our relationship with God. We see our lack of knowledge and understanding on certain subjects as gaps in getting close to God, but He sees them as opportunities. Sometimes what we see as roadblocks, God sees as shortcuts—because now He gets to be the One to help us discover fresh things about Him for the very first time.

Your gaps don't make you less-than. On the contrary. Just like my gaps created special connection points with Guy, your gaps can be shortcuts to closer connection with God.

Breaking Through Roadblocks

What are the roadblocks that you feel stand in the way of having a real relationship with God in this specific season? Perhaps you've noted gaps in your knowledge or gaps in your routines. You're not the first one. There was a woman Jesus met in John 4 who also thought there were too many roadblocks for her to have a real connection with Him. Because of her culture, her background, her heartbreaking past, and her physical location, she thought there was too much standing in the way of having a relationship with God. Jesus meets her by a well she is drawing water from, and He tries to get to know her, reveal to her who He is, and invite her into a relationship with Him. And yet she keeps bringing up . . . roadblocks.

She brings up four.

- She is not the right person (v. 9).
- Hers are not the right circumstances (vv. 11–12).
- Her past is too messy (v. 17).
- She's not in the right place (vv. 19–20).

In fact, the last roadblock is literally about her physical location.

She tells Jesus she's a Samaritan, not a Jew, not part of the people who were understood to be God's chosen people. "Our fathers worshiped here on this mountain," she says, "but Your people say that Jerusalem is the only place for all to worship. *Which is it?*"[1]

She's not crazy. She is repeating what the culture has told her. She is saying she is not in the right *physical* place to encounter God. And she is saying she's not in the right *spiritual* place either.

She is saying she doesn't come from the right background, her past puts her at a disadvantage, and who she is and what she's been through all stand in the way of a real relationship with God.

Have you ever faced those roadblocks?

What about these?

- God doesn't want me. I'm a mess.
- I don't have the right temperament for this.
- I don't have the right personality.
- I could never be close to God. I have done some things—things others don't even know about. I am never telling anyone.
- I can never heal from the hurt that's been done to me.
- I can never experience God the ways others do.
- I don't have the right learning style.
- I don't have the time others do.
- I am not the right person. I don't have the right circumstances. My past is too messy. I'm not in the right place.

I've heard these reasons listed as roadblocks time and time again. Throughout my life, throughout my friendships, and throughout a thousand conversations with new friends as I was writing this book. And I want you to know: You are not crazy. You have real reasons to believe what you do. Culture can make you feel less-than. Your religious upbringing can make you think there's no hope for you. It can feel like everything around you confirms what you've assumed all along: that a relationship with God is good for some people but not possible for you.

And yet, Jesus.

Jesus reveals to this woman what He wants to reveal to you. Yes, there are roadblocks. But Jesus has come to make a way through them. And what He is actually looking for from you might be different from what you've been told.

Jesus says to the woman at the well:

> "The time is coming—it has, in fact, come—when what you're called will not matter and where you go to worship will not matter. It's who you are and the way you live that count before

> God. Your worship must engage your spirit in the pursuit of truth. That's the kind of people the Father is out looking for: those who are simply and honestly *themselves* before him in their worship. God is sheer being itself—Spirit. Those who worship him must do it out of their very being, their spirits, their true selves, in adoration."[2]

The woman replies that she is waiting for the Messiah, the Savior who will one day come and explain everything.

Jesus responds, "I am He."

She puts her faith in Him. She tells her town about Him. Many come to learn that Jesus is available to them, too, and they learn about the way to have a real relationship with God.

Jesus is the ultimate shortcut to God.

Though our sin and shame have separated us from God, once we put our faith in Jesus, we can have a real relationship with God. All we have to do is believe in Him.[3] Though we have encountered roadblocks, Jesus is "the way and the truth and the life."[4] Once we understand this, we can discover it's not as complicated as we've been led to believe.

I don't know what you've been told up until this point. But the time has come when what you are called—the labels others have given you and the boxes others have put you in—does not matter. The place you go to worship does not matter: the geographical location of your feet, the kind of building you're in, the ground you're standing on, the pew you're sitting in, the couch you're lying on. Whether you attend the historic church with stained glass windows or the church that meets in a community-center room with cracked windows is not relevant to qualifying for a real relationship with Jesus.

Instead, it's who you *really* are and how you *really* live that count, according to Jesus Himself.

Remember: God is looking for "those who are simply and honestly *themselves* before him in their worship."[5]

Jesus is saying that true worship is not external; it's internal. It's not about being on this mountain or in that city. It's not about being in that building or having those routines. True worship is not about a place; it is about your inner being glorifying God.

God wants a relationship with the real you. God does not want a relationship with a pretend version of you. God does not want to heal what you pretend to go through. God does not want to answer the prayers you think you're supposed to pray.

God does not want a relationship with a pretend version of you.

God is not looking for people with picture-perfect pasts or impressive lifestyles or titles. He is looking for people who are honestly themselves before Him in worship, engaging in both spirit and in truth.

The enemy of your soul wants you to believe you're not enough, you don't have the time, and you're not the right make and model of a person created to truly know God. He wants you to focus instead on every reason why this peace-filled, healing, and holy relationship is not for you.

Because he knows something you need to know too.

There are not just roadblocks.

There are also shortcuts to God.

Remember what you think of as a gap? God sees it as an opportunity.

If you think your personality is a roadblock, you might be surprised to discover that the God who created you and made you *with* your personality sees it as a shortcut straight to Him.

You might think that the way that you learn, process, or rest is a roadblock. Maybe you're walking through grief, battling loneliness, or overwhelmed by small children, and assuming these roadblocks are in your way when it comes to connecting with Jesus. But what if they're shortcuts directly to His heart?

I asked a thousand people about their roadblocks, and they shared many things as the cause of their spiritual gaps—things that made it hard to feel connected to God. But by far, these six things were the most common:

- Busyness
- Distractions
- Grief
- Shame
- Silence
- Expectations

We're going to take a closer look at each of these roadblocks in part 2 of this book. And then in part 3, we'll unpack the shortcuts—the ways that God has set you up for success to know Him, enjoy Him, know yourself, and enjoy your life with Him. Ways that will reveal that even if you have gaps in your relationship with God, the journey to fill them will be one of the most engaging, fun, challenging, and exhilarating experiences of your life.

After all, it was never about what you know or what you do; it was always about who you are with and how this journey will bring you closer together.

What a relief.

There will be no trivia.

Just ways to break through barriers and discover how you've already been uniquely designed to enjoy God in your real life, right now.

Part 2

Roadblocks

CHAPTER 5

Busyness

"I DON'T HAVE ENOUGH TIME."

Out of over one thousand conversations, busyness was by far one of the most common roadblocks between people and their relationships with God. I wish I could quote each person to you, but that would be an entire book in and of itself. But I wonder if you can relate to any of these snippets from my new friends:

"I am busy taking care of my elderly mom, making dinner, and always making the responsibility of being a mother, wife, and daughter my top priorities. By the time I get quiet time at ten p.m., after all the things are done, I'm exhausted. I can't see straight to read my devotional or the Bible." That's from my new friend who is fifty-one and has been a caregiver for years.

A thirty-seven-year-old hairstylist said her greatest roadblock is "finding the time with my little kids." A fifty-eight-year-old office manager said that his biggest barrier is "changes in my schedule. I know my time with the Lord is supposed to be best in the morning, but my mornings have changed." A twenty-four-year-old fitness instructor also talked about her "chaotic schedule" and the hustle of just trying to pay the bills. A fifty-three-year-old real estate agent can relate. He told me, "It's hard when I have a constant need to be productive with every minute of the day to get everything done. I can't connect until the to-do list is done."

I heard over and over about the very real, nonstop chaos of schedules, responsibilities, and all that comes with caring for relationships, families, and kids.

"I'm tired. I am a parent, I have employees, I am a boss, I have a boss, I'm a homeowner, a volunteer, and a caregiver to a child with chronic disease," said a probation officer.

And a sales director in her mid-fifties asked the million-dollar question: "When you have a family of three kids and all their activities, how do you still make time with God?"

That is a great question. That is the right question.

If God created us to be in a relationship with Him *and* called us to these very time-demanding seasons and tasks, then there *must* be an answer, right? After all, He hasn't set us up for failure. He has set us up for success. So let's ask the questions.

Why do we feel so busy?

Why are we so distracted?

What can be done?

Busyness and distraction might feel like they are exactly the same roadblock, but they have some differences. We will hit on distractions in the next chapter, but first I want to talk about feeling *busy*. Why is busyness one of the greatest roadblocks between us and God? Are we *truly* too busy? Or do we just *feel* too busy? And how can we tell the difference?

You're Not a Cat; You Don't Have Multiple Lives

In all my conversations, I discovered one staggering spiritual snag: We've completely divorced time spent with God from the time we spend doing all the things God has called us to do. And so now we see our charismatic kids, our aging parents, our friends, our siblings, our class schedules or our nine-to-five jobs as competitors for our time. And we view actions like prepping meals, talking with friends, doing the chores, driving the carpool, filing the taxes, and chaperoning at summer camp as being in competition with our relationship with God. Perhaps you've said things like, "I can't get up earlier and read my Bible right now or go to a small group because I'm exhausted from sleepless nights with tiny kids or staying up late dealing with teenager tensions, traumas, and toiletries." And yet why do we think being a good parent or loving friend is at odds with following God?

In what ways might the enemy of our souls be making us feel guilt and shame about our schedules, our commitments, and our relationships, when through them we are, in fact, *obeying God*?

Why do we think being a good parent or loving friend is at odds with following God?

The Word of God says, "Trust in the Lord and do good; dwell in the land and enjoy safe pasture."[1] This means to put the weight of your trust and dependence on God. And while you put your faith in Him, not in yourself, *do good*. Do good where you are. Do good in big ways and small ways, in seen ways and unseen ways. And dwell in the land where God has put you. Instead of thinking ahead to the next season, seize the season you're in. Instead of wanting to hurry to the *next* place, dwell well in *this* place. And rest in God's faithfulness and safety. Rest in knowing the character of God. Rest in remembering the provision of God—right where you are.

How is being faithful in the land where God has put you—your carpool, cubicle, or kitchen—*not* obeying and spending time with God?

How is watching your kids play soccer, helping your parents move, assisting your spouse with a project, nursing the baby at midnight, or being a responsible employee, leader, pastor, or coach *not* obeying and spending time with God?[2]

Whether you are overwhelmed at work (doing things God has called you to do) or exhausted at home (loving those God has called you to love), it can be easy to feel too busy to spend time with God the way that we want to or think we're supposed to. Sure, it's also entirely possible that we have poor organizational skills or have said yes to too many things, and our feelings of overwhelm are a by-product. One hundred percent—that's possible. But many of us don't have poor scheduling skills; we have poor theology. We think the things God has given us to be faithful in are somehow at odds with being faithful to Him.

I think about the brutal weeks this past year when my little brother, Elijah, was in the hospital. We weren't sure what the outcome would be, and during that time I was flying back and forth from speaking events all over the country to be with him in his hospital room for half the week, every week.

I remember thinking, *I can't be the perfect boss.* And I wasn't. I wasn't the most efficient at my professional tasks as I could have been.

I can't be the perfect friend, I thought. And I wasn't. I missed a friend's wedding. I missed two baby showers. I missed visiting a best friend's baby. I missed birthdays. I missed so . . . many . . . texts. I had friends confront me about my absence with them. I let people down. I wasn't as attentive as I had previously been.

And I felt like I wasn't spending enough time with God because I was spending so much time with my brother. *I can't wake up early enough to thoughtfully read my Bible and get to the hospital as soon as visiting hours start. I can't find enough gaps in between doctor visits and things going wrong and taking walks with Elijah around the hospital once he has energy. I can't find a private place to pray in this hospital. When I have any quiet time at all, I am exhausted and can't focus.*

I quickly felt like I wasn't doing anything right in my life.

I wish I'd known then what I know now: that the guilt and shame I felt were not coming from God.

Why was I letting the enemy make me feel bad for loving my brother well?

Why was I letting myself feel guilty for not waking up even earlier for a few weeks to read, and not having time in prayer for as long as I was used to, when I was in fact *doing good* and *dwelling well*?

If I was indeed busy, I was busy doing what God had called me to do. So instead of saying I was *busy*—which sometimes implies a person isn't present or is distracted and overwhelmed—I started to say I was *full*. I was full of being faithful in the land where God had placed me. Sometimes I was distracted and overwhelmed, for sure, but I would not define that season of my life as too busy to encounter God. Instead, I now see how I was full of encountering God in an entirely new way. I was not pulled away by *busyness*. When I chose to bring God into my experiences and see them from His perspective, I was brought even closer to Him through the *fullness*.

Now, let's talk about you.

Why do you think that when you're being present as a parent, you're not following God? You're obeying God. You're loving like God. You're being faithful in the land where He put you.

Why do you think that as you're leading the project God entrusted you with, you're not following God? Are you doing things against God's will? Are you doing things dishonestly? Or are you obeying God? Are you loving like God? Are you being faithful in the land where He has put you?

Perhaps you *are* taking on too much. Perhaps you *are* doing things you're not called to do. Perhaps you *are* doing what God has called you to do, but you are doing it for more hours than He's called you to do it. We can discuss that later.

But first I want to free you from the lie that you have two lives:

1. Your God life.
2. Your real life.

The only way to have a real relationship with God is to have one with Him in the middle of your real life. Everything else is shallow religion. Everything else is faking it. Everything else is putting on a show, a theatrical act we think God wants but He actually disdains. Everything else is legalistically checking boxes, doing what we think we must do, even when those things aren't actually bringing us closer to God.

The only way to have a real relationship with God is to have one with Him in the middle of your real life.

You may think the way to love God best is to have perfectly scheduled time set aside with Him (and for you in this season, maybe that's possible and maybe it isn't). You may think the way to love God best is to have Scripture memorized (and for you in this season, maybe that's possible and maybe it isn't). You may think to love God best is to attend more community events, church services, conferences, or weekly small groups (and you know what I'm gonna say—for you in this season, maybe that's possible and maybe it isn't).

I'm not here to dictate what God might be calling you to in this season. Whatever He's calling you to: Do it.

I do want to put the words of Jesus in front of you though: "In the same way I loved you, you love one another. This is how everyone will recognize that you are my disciples—when they see the love you have for each other."[3]

Following *Jesus* well looks like loving *people* well.

Don't allow the enemy to make you feel as though you can't encounter God in the exact place He has put you.

You've been set up for success. That means your *personality*. That means your *season*. That means *with* your parents. Your kids. Your in-laws (yes, even them). Your classmates. Your church. Your sports team. Your place of work.

Friend, you may have guilt about something you were never meant to have guilt about. The enemy may want you to feel that your season is a roadblock to a relationship with God when in fact it's a shortcut. A shortcut to experience God in a way you've never experienced Him before.

Following *Jesus* well looks like loving *people* well.

Perhaps understanding more about God as a loving parent happens as you lovingly parent your kids, doing things for them they don't even know about, caring for them in ways they can't comprehend, and seeing more clearly how God loves you this same way.

Perhaps you will unlock moments to talk to God while washing the dishes or folding the laundry, discovering the permission you have to turn ordinary moments into altars of praise.

Perhaps you will unearth the beauty of a God who is happily in the details of what He creates as you meticulously work on your new art piece or new work project, and ruminate on how much time God must have spent creating and caring for your details as well. I don't know what this looks like for you in your season of life. But perhaps inviting God into these busy, messy, everyday moments and asking Him to give you His lens in them will help you learn how to see God in your life in ways you haven't before. Perhaps the season you felt was pulling you away can actually pull you in closer to Him than ever before.

It's No Beach, but It's Better

I sat down with a fun-loving mom of four to ask her how she connects with God, especially amid the busyness of raising her children. I had met her at a church where I'd taught months before in Temecula, California, and she had stood out from the crowd. She had a calm confidence about her. She made noticing people and loving people seem easy. Whether she was filling up her plate with food, almost spitting it out as she laughed, or helping put things away as someone was sharing their story with her—only to stop cleaning to hug that person and pray for them, her hands still filled with sticky plates and a tower of napkins—she wasn't rushed. She wasn't overwhelmed. She didn't seem to be overthinking or self-conscious about anything. Being present seemed so natural. I assumed this woman spent her days kneeling at the altar at church for hours on end, with the kind of quiet strength and chill vibe she had. *Surely*, I thought, *she has nothing else to do in her schedule beyond prayer and her skincare routines.*

Then I overheard someone ask her about her four kids. I was shocked. "*Four* kids?"

She smiled and laughed as she nonchalantly went to throw away the Leaning Tower of Plates.

As I was finishing up this chapter, I asked to meet her on a Zoom call. I explained my goal of having a thousand conversations, and I practically begged her to be one, to please share with all of us how she is able to connect with God and juggle all those kids while being so present and so filled with easy joy. I could tell that she personally knew Him. So I asked her: *How?*

She shared that she had had her first kid at twenty-seven, and up until then her time with God had looked like driving to sit on the beach to spend time with Him, praying and reading His Word, sometimes for hours. At home she'd make tea, light a candle, and carve out an equal amount of time in the coziness of her living room. "It seemed like I had all the time in the world," she said with a laugh.

But after her second kid she grew overwhelmed with the busyness of being a mom. She battled fatigue and exhaustion as well as feelings of guilt—feeling as though she wasn't spending enough time with God or perhaps her relationship with Him wasn't as good as it used to be. She didn't have a problem comparing her relationship with other people's relationships with God. She struggled with comparing herself with a past version of herself. She was used to time with God being easy, and when it wasn't easy, she thought something might be wrong.

One night while lying in bed, praying to God to help her with all the guilt and overwhelm she was carrying, one verse kept coming to mind: "My grace is sufficient for you, for my power is made perfect in weakness."[4] By meditating on this verse, she strongly sensed God's message to her: "This is going to look different for you and Me. But My grace is sufficient for you. And My power is made perfect in your weakness." She thought, *God is not mad at me. God is pursuing me.* And it changed her perspective on her current season and all the seasons that were soon to come.

"When I would sit on the beach with God, it was like a Hallmark movie. It was like a perfect depiction of time with someone you love," she said, laughing. "But it was all segmented time. It was the time I designated to spend with God. Now it's all the time. Now it's knitted in throughout my days. Now it's me waking up and saying, 'God, I invite You into this day.' God is in the car with me and my kids. He's with me everywhere I go. I bring Him into every little area and every big area. It's an ongoing conversation. He doesn't just want us to sit with Him sometimes. He wants to be involved all the time. And my relationship with God is more real to me now than ever."

She paused, smiled, and then said, "God showed me He's very flexible." Then we laughed. I loved that.

While we often put pressure on ourselves to have a perfect, set-aside time with God every day, God loves to be a part of all of our day.

She continued describing how what was once a wall ended up being an open door to understanding. "My kids come to me to be nourished, to be comforted, and when they want to have fun. And I realized that's how God thinks of us. He wants us to come to Him with everything we feel and everything we need. He doesn't just want designated time. He wants to hear from us and to be with us all the time."

What made her life *full* also made it possible for her to encounter God in a new way.

What would it look like for you to see the responsibilities, relationships, and real emotions God has given you as shortcuts to experiencing Him in a more real and intimate way than you ever have before? What would it look like to release the guilt of busyness that does not come from God and to invite Him into the fullness of your days? What would it look like to stop trying to experience God in one specific way—as if there were only *one right way*—and invite God into every aspect of your crammed-calendar-tower-of-laundry-too-many-house-projects-and-too-many-deadlines life? Because whatever your life looks like right now, you have permission to meet God right in the midst of it. Not just permission, but an invitation. God is pursuing you. He's very flexible. And being with you in every part of your real life is His absolute favorite.

CHAPTER 6

Distractions

"I CAN'T FOCUS."

"I can't connect with God because of the hustle and bustle of this fast-paced world we live in. Distractions with electronics and people constantly texting or calling, and I don't have a plan of how to connect," said my new forty-nine-year-old friend who is a mom in Oregon.

"My mind tends to wander. I have a hard time suppressing other thoughts during prayer." That's from my new twenty-four-year-old friend who is a graduate student in Massachusetts.

One group of high school friends echoed the same roadblock: "In all honesty, I don't feel like I'm good at connecting with God. My mind wanders when I pray." "The problem is having too many things on my mind." "Distractions like my cell phone get in my way of connecting with God."

A thirty-three-year-old gentleman who is a nurse from Michigan said, "It's hard finding extended periods of time to spend with God. My guilt says I need longer extended time with God than what I've been doing. Also my own mental distractions seem to flood my brain when spending time with God and just get in the way."

Do any of these thoughts sound familiar to you? After hundreds of conversations echoing this one familiar thing, it's hard to ignore: We are some distracted people.

Are we done for? Is there no way to encounter God in a world filled with notifications, Netflix, and noisy neighbors? Since our culture is not conducive to a peaceful mind or a quiet spirit, is our only choice to conform to the pace of the world and give up on having a real relationship with God and a purpose-filled life?

No. *Thank God.*

Our fast-paced culture may not set us up for success. But we do not have to live on autopilot, racing with the rest of the people around us. We have tools available at our fingertips to help us. If we have authority over principalities and dark forces,[1] then we most certainly have authority over our devices. Culture will never set you up to seamlessly, successfully follow God. But here's the good news: When God created the world, He weaved into its fabric all we would need to encounter Him. Around you and within you, you have what you need to encounter God.

I want to unpack for you some things I wish someone would have told me earlier:

- Not all distractions are bad.
- Jesus was distracted. (*What!?*)
- The distractions that steal from you can be managed.
- You can take back your life.

Not All Distractions Are Bad

"My mind keeps getting distracted, and I find myself thinking of other things. I try to begin again from the top."

For weeks, I could not shake this one story from a vibrant and cheerful woman in her early forties. Her words echoed in my mind. I heard a variation of this roadblock time and time again. "I get lost in thought." "My mind goes to a million other places." "I need to restart." I could quote literally hundreds more. Many of us feel distracted in prayer. Our minds wander. Our to-do lists keep growing. Our worries flood our thoughts. We need to be strapped down, isolated, and brainwashed into repeatedly reciting focused liturgies!

Just kidding.

But why do some of us actually imagine a version of that? Why do we have our own versions of "I try to begin again from the top"?

What does "the top" look like for you?

What does the correct way to pray sound like to you?

What kind of prayer do you think God is looking for?

The truth is that God wants to have a conversation with the real you—where you really are and what you're really thinking about.

My point? I don't think unfocused prayers are to be dismissed.

Perhaps you can pray on what's distracting you.

At best, the Holy Spirit is leading your thoughts toward something He wants you to invite Him into. At best, God is leading you into a holy detour with this distraction.

At worst, it's your restless mind going multiple places . . . and *still*, God wants to go there with you. Remember, God doesn't want you to separate your life with Him from the rest of your life.

Even if He's not the one leading you on your wild-thought roller coaster, He wants to join you on the ride.

This happened to me this week. I sat to pray, but my mind immediately starting running a million miles a minute. I thought of my friend whose mom just entered hospice. I prayed for her and her mom. It made me think of my other friend who lost her mom last year, and she's hosting multiple families right now due to a natural disaster in her area. I know she just started a Meal Train. I prayed for her and those families. I then remembered that I had to shoot an email to my publisher, so I began thinking about a dozen other work things and said a prayer for him. "God, help him love this book." (Just kidding.) I started thinking about our last conversation, which was about basketball. *Shocker.*

God doesn't want you to separate your life with Him from the rest of your life.

I started thinking about my brother, who loves basketball. He was diagnosed with an illness we had never heard of before this past year, and out of all the serious things this disease brought, one personal loss for him was being told he could no longer play basketball. I started praying for Elijah. It's been a very hard season. I remembered a friend who lost her dad a year ago this month. I prayed for her. She and her husband have been so kind and encouraging to me, so I thanked God for them. Also a girl who used to work on their church staff recently moved, and I wondered how she was doing. I prayed for her. Out of nowhere, I thought about a hard conversation I had on the calendar. I knew it wouldn't be fun, so I prayed for wisdom for that. Out of the blue again I thought of a project I was a bit behind on, so I prayed for God's help with time management. I prayed for the people working on it with me. *Oh, my family is coming over for dinner tonight!* I thought. So I prayed for my family. *Oh, I wonder if we have avocados! Is it avocado season? Oh, and I need seasoning! Is that the laundry alarm going off?*

Lord God, please help.

This is a (very) shortened version of my rambling thoughts during prayer this week. I was distracted, but by the grace of God, I was able to take this roadblock and turn it into a shortcut—a pathway to pray for whatever was coming to my mind. For the things I was anxious about, I felt a new peace. I was glad to thank God for the people who came to mind. I was glad to pray for those I remembered were going through hard seasons. I took the detour, and it turned into a shortcut to God and what He cares about too.

I texted every person I had thought of, which started life-giving text conversations that continued throughout the week. I remembered to donate to the Meal Train for my friend hosting multiple families. I am so glad I didn't forget. Then I went to switch my laundry and get some avocados in Jesus' name.

When this happens to you, the enemy wants you to feel like your time with God doesn't count, wasn't good, and you need to . . . *start from the top.*

(Start from where you are.)

Here's what I would encourage you to do instead: *Start from where you are.*

Start from where you are and allow God to lead your thoughts—or take Him with you wherever they lead.

What we once thought was a roadblock may be a shortcut after all.

Jesus Was Distracted (*What!?*)

Jesus knew who He was and what He was called to do. In that sense, He was focused. He was focused on God and fulfilling the mission God had called Him to. But make no mistake; along the way, Jesus was distracted.

While Jesus was taking His students—His disciples—to Jerusalem, a man who was blind asked Jesus to help him see. Jesus *stopped* and healed the man.[2] As He continued to travel, He saw a man named Zacchaeus in a tree. Zacchaeus was short, shady, and shunned by many, but Jesus announced He would be going over to his house for a meal.[3] Both men—both distractions—then followed Jesus.

Jesus had a destination, but He was more focused on who He was called to be and what He was called to do. These distractions were welcomed.

There's another story where Jesus lost someone He loved and just needed space. John the Baptist, His cousin, had been killed, and Jesus "got on a boat and went away to spend some time in a private place. The crowds, of course, followed Jesus on foot from their cities. *Though Jesus wanted solitude,* when He saw the crowds, He had compassion on them, and He healed the sick *and the lame.*"[4]

Here, Jesus was grieving. He had every right to want to be alone. And yet His compassion led Him to embrace that interruption.

I could name so many more times in Scripture when Jesus embraced a detour, but here is my point: None of these encounters were on the agenda. But they *did* line up with what God had called Jesus to do. And obeying God was His calling. It is yours too.

You may feel like your kid coming home crying because of something that happened at school is distracting. You may feel like your spouse's frustrations with work are distracting. You may feel like people in your life needing to hop on unexpected calls is distracting. *But not all distractions are bad.*

Jesus followed the distractions that lined up with His calling. And if you are sensitive to God's leading in your life, you will too.

But this is important: Even though Jesus was often moved with compassion and open to distractions, He didn't let everyone's desires and demands derail Him.

In the story where Jesus was grieving John and set out to be alone, He embraced the interruptions from those around Him. He then went to feed over five thousand people who were hungry. He was not just interrupted; He was greatly impactful. And then, immediately "after the crowd had gone, Jesus went up to a mountaintop alone *(as He had intended from the start)*. As evening descended, He stood alone on the mountain, praying."[5]

I love this! Jesus embraced an interruption but still knew He needed rest and alone time with God. That moment was on pause while He obeyed God in another way, but it was not derailed. It was not forgotten. *Resting and spending alone time with God was also obeying God.* Jesus changed the schedule's order, but He still made it a priority to do both. You and I can too.

The Distractions That Steal from You Can Be Managed

It might feel like there's no way to manage the distraction of our devices, but there is. The pace around you does not have to determine the pace within you.

I love Paul's words when he said, "I'm trying to be helpful and make it as easy as possible for you, not make things harder. All I want is for you to be able to develop a way of life in which you can spend plenty of time together with the Master without a lot of distractions."[6]

The pace around you does not have to determine the pace within you.

That is my heart for you as well. I want to help you develop a way of living on purpose, *with* purpose, without distractions ruling your life. If your devices are pulling you away from God and the fullness He's called you to in this season, here are a couple of simple things you can do. This is not an extensive list, but I have found it to be helpful in my own life.

1. Decide

Consider and decide for yourself how much time you want to spend on your phone, watching TV, or with whatever devices that feel like distractions. You likely won't arrive at your destination unless you decide exactly where you want to go. Decide.

2. Design Your Devices Around the Life You Want

After you decide on a goal, create environments that set you up for success by customizing your devices to help you with your goals.

- If notifications constantly distract you, turn them off. If only certain people need to be able to get ahold of you at all times, utilize the Do Not Disturb or Focus options to customize whose texts or calls can come through.
- Determine which apps on your phone are not helpful, and consider limiting your access to them to solely your laptop.
- Try an app that monitors screen time and enforces app boundaries. Research a few options and try them out. For some of us, the tools in our phones and computers may be enough. Make the time to use the tools that can help you live the life you've decided on.

3. Designate

If you are distracted in prayer because you keep grabbing your phone, set your phone somewhere else. Perhaps leave it in another room, or place it somewhere out of your line of sight. As simple as it sounds, removing it from your visual field helps remove the distraction. And if that is not possible, put it on Do Not Disturb.

4. Don't Close the Windows

Sometimes we crave silent moments or opportunities to talk to God, but as soon as we have them, we fill them. We scroll through them. Instead, this week, while you're in a grocery line waiting your turn, notice the window of time and talk to God in your heart. While you are driving to pick something up, maybe don't put on music for the first half, and instead talk to God. Maybe listen to a sermon on a podcast, or the Bible on audiobook. I don't know what your windows look like. But I encourage you to look for them and then keep them wide open to God.

5. Don't Just Digital Detox

Digital detoxes can be very helpful. And yet, when you put up a temporary, uber-strict boundary against the digital world, only to later overindulge when you get back on your technology, the process can be very *un*helpful. Don't just abstain and then binge. The goal is not to do the most extreme thing possible. The goal is to find a sustainable rhythm and pace that helps you keep living with joy, connection, and purpose in your real life. Use a digital detox not as a punishment or a fleeting fad but as a way to help you create sustainable, healthier habits for the long haul.

6. Do Things That Give You Real Joy and Real Meaning

Sometimes we go to our phones for a moment of escape or entertainment. This provides a hit of dopamine—a chemical that chats between the brain and the body's nerve cells and gives us temporary pleasure. Since dopamine gives us a temporary rush but does not last long, by nature it can become addictive. This is often why we pick up our phones or open social media without thinking about or even truly desiring it.

But engaging in activities that bring us *real joy* produces a different chemical, serotonin, which creates lasting feelings of happiness, well-being, meaning, calm, and contentment. With low levels of serotonin, we may see negative impacts in our mood, our reactions to people or circumstances, and our overall sense of happiness. At times, we may be tempted to seek out dopamine as a quick fix for those negative feelings, although that fix won't last.[7] Enter: our epidemic of not just being distracted but choosing to pick up our distractions.

The solution to a distracted life is not to just *stop* going to things that eat up your time. The solution is to *replace* those things with other activities that bring the joy and peace and satisfaction you truly crave.

So the question is, *What brings you real joy?*

Health experts will tell you that moving your body and being out in the sun are two of the quickest surefire ways to increase serotonin.[8] That's a great place to start. Positive neuroscientists will tell you that social connection, whether through intentional, meaningful time with one friend, or a lively time with a group of friends where the time seems to pass by quickly, is also an excellent way for your serotonin levels to rise and for you to feel especially present.[9] Those are excellent places to look as well. Perhaps there are hobbies you once loved that brought you satisfaction and contentment that you can pick up again. Perhaps you want to start adding in more walks, time outside, or planning both sacred and silly times with loved ones. I don't know what brings *you* the most genuine joy in *your* season, but I know that science has caught up with what the Word of God tells us: "Be careful how you live; *be mindful of your steps* . . . Make the most of every *living and breathing* moment because these are evil times."[10]

Both science and the Word of God are saying, Consider how you want to spend your life. There is no one-size-fits-all prescription for every single person in every single season with every single screen. I won't tell you how to lead your family or lead your soul. But I want you to read God's Word and take it seriously. Examine your life and determine if you are living the life you want to live. Are you living with true, lasting joy?

Consider how you want to spend your life.

Here are some of the solutions shared by the one thousand friends I talked to about overcoming the roadblock of distraction.

"I have found that I have to connect first thing in the morning before I start anything else, even if it's for just a few minutes. I also started writing Scripture and doing a journal at night. Writing my prayers also helps me to focus."

"I used to think I 100 percent needed to be seated at my kitchen table with my Bible open, but as I've gotten closer to God, I've realized that I can close the figurative door to the secret place anywhere. Now I connect with Him in the car driving over my favorite bridge, and on walks."

"I used to hate doing laundry. I used to hate how much time it took and all it took me away from. Now I pray over all the laundry that I fold—for who will be wearing the clothes and what they will go through during the week. I use my time folding laundry as a time of prayer, a time of just me and God, and my time with Him has never been better. It's changed laundry and it's changed prayer for me."

I love that last one. Something she used to consider a distraction she now uses as time to spend with God. We can do the same. We don't have to live distracted, depleted, and then feeling so much shame that we go back to the things that distract and deplete us. If we are mindful of our steps, we can take back our time, take back our joy, and take back our lives.

We Can Take Back Our Lives

One sweet gentleman's story opened my eyes to the importance of taking back our time. He'd recently entered his retirement era and confessed that he'd been a workaholic, but he'd justified that choice as the family provider, chalking his busyness up to love. He assumed that once he was retired, he would finally be able to go deeper in his relationship with his family and also with God. But he quickly found other ways to fill up his time—other reasons why he needed to take on new projects, other endeavors he needed to start. He'd put off time with God and family until the fourth quarter of his life, only to realize if he wasn't careful, he would put it off forever.

So he made a choice to change his priorities and his pace. He was worried at first that his life would feel like it got overhauled. Instead he noticed there were just small adjustments that needed to be made. Doing the same projects, but doing them slower, with kids and grandkids. Going fishing, but now quietly talking to God on his boat. Reading a couple of verses a few times a week and discussing them with his wife on walks. The fourth quarter of his life hasn't changed everything about him, but his posture toward God has changed in everything he does. He smiled as he said, "I'm very happy with this change."

Don't believe the lie that one day there will be no distractions. My retired friend will tell you he wishes he'd enjoyed his life with God and with others earlier, and he is so very glad he made the small but significant changes to take back his life now. You can too.

CHAPTER 7

Grief

"I'M HURTING TOO MUCH."

"Okay, you can say *one* bad word right now, but no more."

I was packing as fast as I could, tears streaming so rapidly that I could hardly see what I was throwing into my suitcase. It was a Wednesday afternoon during my freshman year of college, and my sister had called me to tell me to come home. Dad was not waking up, and I needed to get on a flight right away.

When I got the call, I had just finished getting a haircut a few blocks away from my dorm room. I had planned to grab lunch and do errands at Target before heading to my afternoon class, not sprint down crooked sidewalks and run across oncoming traffic as fast as I could to get on the first plane out. As I burst into my room, I was overcome with emotion.

How much time do I have? Should I just go to the airport without packing? What if he dies? Do I pack something black? What if he wakes up and I stay all week? Grab laptop for possible homework. Grab dress for possible funeral. No time.

I was shouting words to myself and to the air in confusion and chaos as I threw something dark (close enough to black) into my suitcase and fell on my knees in front of my closet, weeping. I screamed, "Please, God, no!" I said an explicit word somewhere in there. I kept crying aloud. One of my roommates fell to the floor with me and wrapped her arms around me, assuring me her boyfriend was pulling the car around to drive me to the airport. A handful of friends ran into the room, helping me pack things that I would have surely forgotten. My dad had been sick for a while. We had prayed for his recovery. We had gathered enough hope for me to return to college.

More friends ran in, telling me my ride had arrived. They double-checked that my ID was in my wallet and that a phone charger was in my bag. Then one of my hallmates walked over to our huddle on the floor and put her hand on my shoulder.

"Okay, you can say *one* bad word right now, but no more. Don't say anything God wouldn't be proud of."

I stood up, embarrassed, and said I was sorry. Then I headed to the airport.

March Twelfth

I will never forget March 12, 2008, the day my dad went to be with Jesus. Out of all Wednesdays ever, it might be the worst Wednesday to ever Wednesday.

I will never forget the people who drove in from all over the Bay Area to be at my childhood home that night and weep with my family. I will never forget the people who would fly from all over the country to mourn with us at my dad's funeral a week later. I will never forget the woman from his church who I hardly knew who offered to take me to the mall and buy a new black dress for me to wear. (It turns out, the blurry dark clothing I packed was not black, and also, it was pajamas.) I will never forget the people who thought of my basic needs that week when I couldn't. Including my college roommates and their boyfriends. Packing my chargers. Leaving class to drive me to the airport. And weeping on the floor with me.

And also, I will never forget what it felt like to feel bad for the words I expressed in my grief.

The roommate who was offended by my explicit word choice was not trying to be cruel. I had become aware of things that offended her early on, and it was good for me—this city kid who was a bit rough around the edges (and said words she didn't even know were controversial or unkind until learning otherwise)—to be more sensitive of others, mindful of my words, and more gracious as a person overall. Truth be told, I needed to grow in these areas. I'd had no idea how some felt about certain words or phrases, and I was actually learning a lot.

But in that moment, all my filters were gone. I was not thinking of the best possible words, much less who was around me. I was crying out to God from the deepest pit of grief. But she was offended, and in that moment, she let me know it. By her standards, one bad word was okay, but no more. And her statement communicated that God's opinion of me, on that brutal day, was one of disappointment—as if He was up in the sky, looking down with a pen and paper in hand, grading my grief, taking notes, deciding if He would still be proud of me or not.

Now, let me pause and say that I am not here to defend or praise harsh language.

But as I processed my grief in the days and months following my dad's death, I kept coming back to that moment. It made me unsure of what I was allowed to say. What was the *holy* thing to say? What words would God approve of me saying in the first month of losing my dad? I wasn't sure what to say to Him or to others. Soon I felt like my grief had become a roadblock between me and God.

I did my best. Was I supposed to say, "Thank You, God, for the years I had with my dad"? Was I supposed to mimic the people I barely knew who attended the funeral and said things like, "God had to take him because He needed another singer in the choir"? Was I supposed to pretend like I was okay? Was I supposed to ask God to help me use this pain to help others? What was the most perfect and godly thing I could say? What *wouldn't* disappoint God? What would God *let* me say? I'd already used up my one-bad-word pass.

We, the Hurting

In talking to over a thousand people, a couple hundred mentioned grief. They mentioned hard seasons. They mentioned heartbreaking circumstances that ripped them away from routines and community, and how they were not in the best place to be close to God. I could relate.

An entrepreneur in her fifties said, "After losing my husband, I have so much more to do around the house and have less time with God than I did before. I struggle with time, especially when I'm more sad."

A retired gentleman in his seventies said, "I feel my words aren't adequate to speak with God. Sometimes I have anger. Sometimes I have questions. Sometimes I don't know what I feel. I don't always have the best words for God."

"I'm stressed from school and applications. It's hard to connect to God when I'm in a season of waiting." That was from a twenty-one-year-old student in Kentucky.

And a fifty-six-year-old nurse from Los Angeles said, "I can't connect with God when I am in a valley. But I will when I'm out of it."

So many of us have felt like our painful seasons have put our relationships with God on hold. We think that once that season is over, and once the therapist's bill is fully paid and we're fully healed, then we will go back to better routines and try to restart. We hope one day we'll be less sad, have more time, and have better words.

We think we need a different life, a different personality, and different words before we can engage with God.

We could not be more wrong.

Jesus' brother James told us, "Come close to the one true God, and He will draw close to you."[1]

As you get more real with God, His presence becomes more real to you. The inverse is also true. The more you refuse to be real with God, the more you distance yourself from Him. God wants to be close to you, but He will not force you to be close to Him. God comes where He is wanted. But if you do not invite Him in, He will not override your choice.

If you want to be close to God, you are invited to—right here, right now. Just as you are.

And the great news?

You don't have to show off for God to show up.

You don't have to have the perfect words. You don't have to pretend that you're someone you're not, or in a place that you're not in. God doesn't want a relationship with a pretend version of you. He wants a real relationship with the real you.

You don't have to show off for God to show up.

The best thing you can do for your well-being, for your soul, for your real life, and for your relationship with God is to tell

Him your doubts. Tell God your fears. Tell God what's breaking your heart. Tell Him the ways you need Him. The Word of God tells us that "God is our shelter and our strength. When troubles seem near, God is nearer, and He's ready to help."[2]

Getting real with God invites the power of God and the peace of God to meet you where you really are.

We *do not* have to pretend like we are not going through hard times. We don't have to hold in our tears, ignore our pain, and just say, "God is good all the time. Nothing is wrong at all." No. Why? Because God *is* good all the time, and He is *so* good that He sent Jesus, Emmanuel, which literally means "God with us." He is with us in our real pain. With us in our real questions. With us on our college dorm-room floors.

The truth? You don't have to edit your prayers.

This may be controversial for some. Perhaps you feel that some words are not appropriate for prayer. After all, God is holy, and unholy words should not be used in the presence of a holy God. And if that's your thought process, I don't think you and I disagree. We should have the fear of the Lord, coming humbly before Him and recognizing the power and the glory of the One we are speaking to—100 percent. But here is also what I have come to discover: In all His power and all His glory, God does not want you to edit what you are truly feeling. He doesn't want a highlight reel that's been edited together with the best moments through flowery filters. That's cute for Instagram. Not cute for God. He wants to meet you where you really are.

You don't have to edit your prayers.

God is not shocked by your grief.

Have you ever lost someone?

God knows what it's like to lose a son.

Have you ever given a lot to someone who never gave anything back?

God knows what it's like to not be loved by those He loves.

Have you ever mourned the loss of a relationship?

God knows what it's like to be close to someone and have them turn their backs on Him.

God is all too familiar with grief. He has felt what we have felt. So He is the last person to dismiss it. He is the last person to condemn you for it. He is the last person to say, "This makes you less like Me." No. Instead, you share grief in common.

Now, once again—just so I don't receive terrible reviews on this book and hate emails in my inbox in valiant defense of my hallmate—I don't think she was wrong to be sensitive. I don't think harsh words are to be glorified. I have no judgment for her here.

But when I think of God's posture toward me in my deep grief—now that I know Him a bit better and know more about His character—I have come to believe He is more like my roommate who fell on the floor weeping with me. I think He's more like her boyfriend who ran out of his class to get his car to drive me to the airport. I think He's more like my friend who bought a plane ticket for me and never let me pay her back. More like my friend in the military who flew across the country on his few days off to be at the funeral with me. More like the woman who thought of my practical needs and bought my dress.

And as I was real with God, He became more real to me. He was closer as I told Him, "I'm mad at You. Dad and I didn't have enough time. I don't know what to do now with my life. I don't know how to comfort my little brother. I don't know who will take care of my mom. I don't want to go back to college. I don't want to do anything without my dad. I'm angry. I miss him so much."

Here's what I have learned: As you get more real with God,

He will become more real to you. As you wrestle *about* God, wrestle *with* God. Bring Him in on your hurts and receive His compassion and love for you as you walk through this painful time. Your relationship with God is not on hold while you grieve.

Yes, at times, grief can be a roadblock to our relationship with God. But it doesn't have to be. Grief can also be a catalyst. When you allow God into the most painful places of your life, it's often those very situations that can help you break through the surface and experience God in a more real and intimate way.

As you wrestle *about* God, wrestle *with* God.

God Is with You

Hundreds shared about times they felt their grief was a roadblock. And hundreds more shared how their grief, painful seasons, and hardships had drawn them closer to God than ever before.

One woman said, "After my husband died, I have learned that lament is a form of prayer that I really didn't use before, and I can connect with God in a whole new way through lament."

"As I have grown older," said a gentleman who recently retired, "I learned the hard way that I need prayer. My divorce brought me closer to God and helped me realize my need for God. It turns out, I'm not perfect. I need God."

"I have filled several notebooks during my divorce, prayed like never before, and never felt closer to God." This was from a life coach in her late sixties.

"I used to think I couldn't connect with God the way I used to because of all the busyness of life's responsibilities. I'm the sole caregiver of my disabled daughter. But now instead of my previous routine, I've become more connected with my small group. They keep me grounded. I connect with God in my time with them," said my new friend in her fifties.

From my sweet new friend in her early forties: "I recently went through a miscarriage. Immediately people started pouring love over me and praying like crazy. It was the first time that I could see and feel God answering prayers one after another, almost instantaneously. I would be a mess on the floor, and then all of a sudden, this peace and joy would wrap around me. And I remember saying, 'That was definitely God! Someone had to have been praying for me just now!' So, prayer has changed for me. I now pray as soon as a person pops into my head or as soon as I start feeling stressful emotions rather than waiting for a 'designated' prayer time."

Then one of my friends in her mid-thirties, from Sydney, Australia, told me when God became more real to her. In her sweet and singsong Aussie accent, she said, "Growing up, I remember feeling the Holy Spirit. I remember people encouraging me to pray in power. I remember big moments with God." Then she moved to LA. Her community, rhythms, and outlook changed. "I had to grow up spiritually. I started to have a daily discipline of time with God. I became obsessed with the Bible, the context of Scripture, and what it all meant." Then there was an immense loss in her life: the end of her marriage. There was profound grief. "Now, I was learning how to have honest conversations with God," she said, "This is when my eyes opened up to God speaking through many other ways . . . ironically through grief. Now, in my grief, in the removal of so much safety, this closeness was real in a whole new way. It wasn't coming from a pastor, or a sermon, or a family member. It was personal. I found God for myself. It was in this place where He became mine."

I love that her relationship with God was constantly evolving and growing in different ways through different seasons. Also, I love that what the enemy could have used to harm her—when she got real with God and surrendered it to Him—God used for His glory and her good. Today, she might be one of the most real, raw, joy-filled, and in-love-with-Jesus-for-real people I know.

As it turns out, you can invite God into the not-so-pretty parts of your life and let your relationship be more real with Him than it's ever been. Getting real with God in your real grief can be one of the most groundbreaking moments of your faith. And that looks like not being fake, that looks like not trying to fit into any sort of formula, that looks like not waiting until your life looks a certain way. Instead, it looks like coming to God with what you're really going through and allowing Him to bring real peace and real comfort to where you really are. When you do that, I believe you, too, will get to a place where your faith does not look like anyone else's or even like any of your past seasons. Instead you will be able to say, "It was in *this* season—in *this* place—where He became mine."

CHAPTER 8

Shame

"I'M NOT GOOD ENOUGH."

I recently joined the #CoolKidsGlassesClub. (I've decided that by calling it cool, it *becomes* cool *in the name of Jesus.)*

It turns out, I was *blind* . . . and nobody told me.

My doctor asked if I could see a particular sign, and I said, "No way. Can *anyone* see that?"

She responded, "Yes, *everyone* can see that . . . except people who need glasses."

Womp womp. I told her she didn't need to worry. "I have lived my whole life without realizing this," I explained, "so I'm sure I'm okay. I am very used to living this way."

"Just because you're used to it doesn't mean it's what's best for you," she said. "Do you find it difficult to do *this* . . . ? Do you struggle in environments like *this* . . . ? Is it hard to see when you're in a room like *this* . . . ?" And as she began to describe what I thought were normal scenarios in my life, I answered, "Yes, I struggle with all of that. But I thought *everyone* lived that way."

And then she said this to me:

"You have been living your whole life with limitations you don't have to live with anymore."

Wow.

And then she prescribed me glasses. So, praise God, everything is new. And turns out, our entire world isn't fuzzy!

Today, I wonder what lens you have been seeing your life through.

Your lens can be formed by your wounds. Perhaps something unjust happened to you. Perhaps something was taken from you. Perhaps your voice was silenced. Perhaps your hopes were shattered.

Your lens can be formed by words. Perhaps hurtful words were spoken over you. Perhaps there were words you longed to hear but no one said. Perhaps there are harmful words you tell yourself over and over.

Your lens can be formed by what you surround yourself with. The things you scroll through online. The people whose opinions you value.

Your lens can be what you've done and your own feelings of inadequacy. The guilt you feel because of that one thing you did. The embarrassment you feel because of those things you said. Your feelings of not making the mark, not being good enough, and needing to do more and try harder to have a good relationship with God. Maybe your lens of faith was a high bar, too far out of reach. Maybe you see yourself as unworthy of having a real relationship with God.

I want you to know what I wish I would have known so much earlier: You may be living with limitations you don't have to live with anymore.

Jesus came to give you a new life *and* a new lens. He wants you to see yourself for who you really are. Why? Because your lens impacts how you live. If you believe you're not enough to be close to God, you'll act like you're not enough. You will start to live a life that is far less than what God has for you. And you're not alone.

Out of over one thousand people I interviewed around the world, shame was one of the main reasons why they felt it was hard to connect with God. Athletes. CEOs. Pastors. Parents. Artists. Seventeen-year-olds. Sixty-eight-year-olds. Couples married for thirty-eight years. Therapists of nineteen years who have helped set others free but can't seem to find freedom themselves. I met the most gracious, kind, vulnerable people who told me how they just can't break through their shame. Here are some of their words. Can you relate?

A forty-six-year-old nurse in Indiana said, "I feel like I can't connect with God if I've done something wrong or shameful that day or week. I live in a lot of guilt."

"Whenever I start to feel worthy, I do something that makes me feel unworthy, and then I'm a mess-up again. I'm just lost." That was my new friend in his mid-sixties who recently retired in Fort Worth, Texas.

This one made me smile: "My biggest walls are all my ungodly behaviors and my ghetto coming out," laughed a forty-four-year-old director in California. She is my people, and since you're reading one of my books, she may be one of your people too.

"I put so much pressure on myself for doing it right, and what my time with God should look like," confessed a lively and beautifully ambitious twenty-three-year-old grad student from Kansas City, Missouri. "I am always afraid I'll do something wrong. I compare myself to others who seem to have all of this connection and all of this healing, and I'm just so behind. It's frustrating."

"I've often thought God doesn't want me. I've done too

much. Maybe one day I can get my life together, but it isn't today. Sometimes I think I have too much I have to fix first," said a most sincere and honest gentleman in his sixties, who worked for the city of San Francisco most of his life.

There were some common themes. Shame for things they wish they hadn't done. Shame for standards they feel like they are not meeting. Shame for not having everything in their lives figured out yet.

Their lenses impacted their lives. They believed they were not enough, so they lived like they were not enough. That's what the enemy of our souls hopes we all believe.

If you can relate to any of their stories, I want you to know: *Just because you've grown used to seeing your story through a lens of shame doesn't mean that's what's best for you.*

You may be living held back by shame—but you don't have to anymore.

The Truth About Shame

I think back to the boy I adored in high school and the family I thought I could never live up to. There were ways I thought I had to live in order to be good enough. And I was shocked to discover that he felt so much shame from comparison that he'd started pretending himself.

He is not alone. One of the enemy's favorite ways to keep us from God is unrelenting guilt and shame. He hopes that we feel not good enough, not worthy enough, and like we are constantly letting God and others down.

The enemy hopes we'll fixate on all the ways we think we are falling short. He hopes we'll feel so much shame that we try to hide from God.

Why? Because he knows that if we stopped hiding, were

honest with God, and came to Him with what we're really carrying, then we would be in the best possible position to have a real relationship with Him.

The enemy hopes we'll fixate on all the ways we think we are falling short.

Shame does not come from God.

Shame is a roadblock.

Since the beginning of time, shame has been the enemy's favorite way of keeping us from God.

In Genesis, in the garden of Eden, we meet the first two humans, Adam and Eve. The enemy came to them in the form of a snake and tried to make them doubt God's words, doubt God's character, and doubt who they were. He tempted them with more power, told them they would be like God if they ate a forbidden fruit. After Adam and Eve believed him, disobeyed God, and ate the fruit, they felt so much shame and their instinct was to hide and then cover themselves up.

If Adam and Eve had been two of the one thousand people I spoke to, I am convinced shame would have been one of their top roadblocks too.

Prior to that moment, they were in a close relationship with God just as they were—naked, exposed, and free, just as God had made them. But now we find them hand-making clothing out of fig leaves.

Enter the first garments in history.

I have a voluptuous fig tree in my backyard; I can see it from the dining room table where I'm currently writing this, as the tree's leafy shade hovers over a picnic table where we often play card games. I have always loved fig leaves and what they remind me of. When I see their larger leaves, I think, *These are what Adam and Eve used to cover up.* They are visual reminders to me that though we think we need to cover up, the truth is the opposite. Hiding does not help our relationship with God. Instead, hiding hurts it.

Like Adam and Eve, when we feel shame, we often cover up.

What are your fig leaves?

Maybe it's pretending you're someone you're not. Posting untrue things about your life online. Speaking untrue things about yourself. Maybe it's putting on a façade to people around you. Perhaps it's pretending like you're okay when you're not. Or maybe you don't try to fake it at all. Maybe you've just resigned yourself to the idea that you'll never be good enough. Perhaps you're not even trying to have a relationship with God because it feels like there's no point. You just don't feel worthy. Your life isn't as put together as you want it to be right now. Perhaps you're running away from God and you're running from people. Perhaps you're so used to seeing yourself through a lens of shame that you've resigned yourself to a life of hiding.

But God did not create us to hide. Hiding from God is an unnatural state for your soul. God created us to live in the light and to live free from anything that would separate us from Him and divide us from each other. That means free from sin, free from guilt, free from insecurity, and free from believing you need to earn God's love. Freedom is the state your soul was meant for.

So God sent a different kind of covering. Something that would last longer than our fig leaves. We thought we needed to be covered? We were right.

"Without the shedding of blood, sin cannot be forgiven."[1]

Enter: Jesus.

Our fig leaves were not sufficient. What man couldn't do, Jesus did.

Jesus died on the cross for us and paid the penalty for our wrongdoings, and His blood now covers our sins. This is the only covering we need. That shame you feel? The debt for those sins has already been paid in full.

"Yes, Adam's one sin brings condemnation for everyone, but Christ's one act of righteousness brings a right relationship with God and new life for everyone."[2]

This isn't about *you* being enough. This is about Jesus being enough to cover your sins.

You may be living in guilt and shame that Jesus already set you free from.

And He did.

So here's the truth: You may be living in guilt and shame that Jesus already set you free from. You may be living with limitations you don't have to live with anymore.

Breaking Free from Shame

There is a difference between guilt and shame.

Guilt can be a gift. Guilt can be a signal to you that something is not right, so then you can fix it. You can say you're sorry. You can forgive that person. You can make sure you don't do that thing anymore.

Guilt is a feeling telling you that something you have done is wrong. Shame is the state of believing that you yourself are wrong.

The apostle Paul told us, "Now *this type of deep sorrow,* godly sorrow, is not so much about regret; but it is about producing a change of mind and behavior that ultimately leads to salvation. But *the other type of sorrow,* worldly sorrow, *often is fleeting and* only brings death."[3]

Guilt can lead us to repentance and healing. When we don't deal with our guilt, it can turn into a life of shame and hiding.

But there is a way to break through the roadblock of shame.

Say It and Share It

John told us, "If we confess our sins, he is faithful and just and will forgive us our sins and purify us from all unrighteousness."[4]

When we keep our sins, our shame, our secrets, and what we are really going through hidden, we will start to live with limitations that we don't have to live with. The enemy does his best work in the dark. He does his best work when we hide. But God gave us a way to be free. Say it out loud—confess it to God. And share it—tell it to a trusted person. That is how we will live whole and healed. That's how you start to live the full life you've been created to live.

And this isn't a onetime event. This is a lifestyle of living free. "Make this your common practice: Confess your sins to each other and pray for each other so that you can live together whole and healed."[5]

There is power in the practice of getting real. The enemy of our souls does not want us to get real with ourselves, get real with God, or get real with others because he knows he will lose his grip when we bring what was once hidden into the light.

Healing and wholeness are possible . . . *in the light.*

Something supernatural happens when you say it and share it.

Curt Thompson, a board-certified psychiatrist, has spent years studying the psychology of shame. He writes that we must "name things to tame things. Simply naming the moment as a shame event shifts our attention, taking us out of its vortex, allowing us to observe it more dispassionately."[6]

There is power in the practice of getting real.

Researcher Brené Brown writes, "The less we talk about shame, the more control it has over our lives."[7] She says that in all her years of researching shame, she has seen it become a wall in relationships. And yet, "Shame happens between people, and it heals between people. . . . Shame loses power when it is spoken."[8]

The Word of God affirms this research. By naming it and saying it out loud, shame's power starts to shrink in your life.

Set aside some time. Five minutes. Twenty-two minutes. Your call. What works for your schedule and will work for your soul? And think about why you feel this shame. Is it one specific thing you did? One specific person you feel you let down? Is it because you used to be able to connect with God but now feel like you're hiding from Him? By naming the thing that makes you feel shame, it begins to lose its power.

Say it. Come out of hiding and tell God how you really feel.

Share it. Tell a trusted person. A spouse. A friend. A safe person at church.

Wholeness and healing are possible on the other side of getting real.

Get Back Up

One of the most memorable of my one thousand conversations was with a friend and athlete from Oklahoma City who lost his lower left leg in 2018. A competitive and immensely talented football player in high school and college, he had multiple scholarship offers, scouts competing for his time, and a shining future ahead of him. Then after one evening of nightclubs, drinking, losing track of his friends, and looking for a pay phone to call his mom, he was crawling under a stopped train when it unexpectedly started to move, and he tripped and hit his head, rendering him unconscious.

Wholeness and healing are possible on the other side of getting real.

When he woke up, his left foot was gone. He told me of the shame he felt in the months that followed. He and his sister were raised by their single mom, and his plan was for his athletic scholarships to pay for his schooling and for his athletic career to ultimately bless back his mom. The first words he said to his mom when he woke up in the hospital room were, "I'm sorry."

He spoke of the shame he felt for the things he could have controlled and the shame he felt for things beyond his control. "I felt like I couldn't go to God. I had so much shame. And I was so angry." He talked of the months he spent depressed, in a really dark place, unsure of what his life would amount to, and all the ways he avoided people and avoided God.

He said his mom didn't shame him though. She kept telling him, "You're going to come back from this."

Then she told him to get up and get back to who she knew he really was. "No one can grow your relationship with God except for yourself," she had said. "No one else can do this for you."

He knew it was time to get back up. He started getting real with God. He started reading the book of Job and said it helped him get closer to God than ever before. He started letting people in. "I could have run from God and run from my friends. And if I didn't reunite with my teammates, this might have been a whole different story. But I let them in. And the love they showed me, and the love my mom showed me, and that God showed me—it changed my life."

He went on to pursue track and field as a para-athlete, and when the Olympics landed in Paris in 2024, he landed as well with his prosthetic leg and a new lease on life. He won two silver medals in the 2024 Paralympic Games, in the high jump F64 and long jump F64.

"What I once thought was the worst, God redeemed for the best," he said. "I've grown more in my faith and in my life than I ever imagined, and I'm still growing. Now I share my story to help other individuals and other amputees and help them with their confidence and in their walk with God too."

For a long time, shame was the lens through which he saw himself. It was once a roadblock that held him back and held him down. But my friend chose to get back up—to let God in and to let people in. Today, he's running, physically and spiritually, with more confidence and freedom than ever before.

I don't know what lens you've seen yourself through. But I want you to know how God sees you:

"Now there is no condemnation for those who belong to Christ Jesus."[9]

God does not shame you. Once you put your faith in Jesus, God sees you through the lens of His Son, Jesus. And Jesus has no sin. Jesus is blameless. There is no condemnation for Jesus. So *now* there is no condemnation for those who belong to Jesus. Now you are in Christ. Everything that applies to Jesus applies to you.

And this is good news for us. This means if you're feeling defeated, weighed down, not enough, and like you just don't have faith in yourself . . . I want you to know that you don't have to have faith in yourself.

You just need to have faith in Jesus.

Do you believe Jesus is enough?

Do you believe His blood is enough to cover your sins?

Do you believe Jesus is worthy?

This has nothing to do with how good you are. This has everything to do with how good Jesus is.

You can choose to put your faith in Jesus and receive God's amazing and powerful forgiveness.

This has nothing to do with how good you are. This has everything to do with how good Jesus is.

You can choose to get back up.

Shame is one of the enemy's oldest roadblocks between us and God. But Jesus is the ultimate shortcut. He is the only way to God. The long and winding road of rules won't get you there. Climbing the mountain of expectations won't get you there. Having the perfect story with no speed bumps won't get you there. But by putting your faith in Jesus, you can have a real, honest relationship with God. And as you continue to get real with Him about all you're carrying and all you're going through, and as you continue to turn from your sins and receive His grace that covers them, you will draw closer to God than ever before.

Today, don't hold back. Don't stay hidden.

Say it and share it. And take the shortcut through shame and run straight to Jesus.

CHAPTER 9

Silence

"I CAN'T HEAR GOD."

She told me she felt God's presence through birds.

I thought, *Oh, boy. This is already going downhill real quick.*

I was sitting with three women in Winter Park, Florida, who had honestly taken my breath away. They had me grinning and giggling as they talked about their daughters' favorite skincare routines, the best concerts they'd been to that year, and what they'd picked out to wear, all the while talking about both the gritty, hard things and the goodness of God in their lives. I thought, *I love these women!*

As we started talking about the real ways we all connect with God, I was so inspired. The women talked about how it's changed throughout different seasons for them. There was a second marriage. There was an unexpected loss. There were a lot of kids. A lot of tears. A lot of laughs. And they shared about how they have had to overcome comparing their relationships with God to other people's (same here) and learn not to judge other people's (same here), and not to succumb to pressure that doesn't come from God (louder for the people in the back).

And then she said it—a woman who I thought was just the nicest and the coolest and most normal—said that she feels the presence of God through birds.

I will raise my hand and admit it to you right now: I instantly judged her (something I just said I was learning to overcome). I thought to myself, *No matter what she tells me, I'm not putting a story of her feeling the presence of God through birds in my book. That's not my lane, not my personality, and not for my people.*

And yet, here we are.

She talked about moments she asked God to confirm ways she was feeling led, and times that she felt peace beyond anything she could understand by the spotting of certain birds in certain situations. Of course, I had follow-up questions. I said, "Were any of those choices the right choices? Do you feel like it was really God?"

"Without a doubt," she said. But more than that, she said she felt a sense of God being so very close to her, no matter what choice she made.

She said, "I know I sound crazy."

I said, "I'm glad you know that."

We all laughed. Again, I had found a girl gang I loved.

After a beat of silence, I asked her another question. It turned out to be an important one. I did not know anything about birds, but I did know something about God. So on the off chance this woman wasn't absolutely losing it, I said, "Is there anything in your early childhood memories, or anything in your early life, where birds became particularly special to you?"

She looked at me, stunned.

"God would never expect me to feel His presence through birds," I continued. "I can't stand birds. I also didn't grow up around a lot of animals. But is there something in *you*—something that would make the God who loves *you* and knows *you* seem close . . . because of a bird?"

She turned in her chair to face me directly, and with tears welling in her eyes, she said, "I have *never* thought of this before in my life!"

Wiping droplets from her cheeks she said, "When I was a little girl, one of my greatest connections to God was through my grandparents. I loved spending time with them. One time a bird flew onto the porch, and my grandpa said, 'Look! That's a sign that God loves you and is close to you. Whenever you see a bird, remember that.'"

We were all silent.

She then repeated, "I've *never* once thought about that!"

We laughed, wiped more tears, and I leaned in, lowering my voice now that we were all in on the bird secret. "Is it possible," I asked, "that this is a unique thing with you and God *because* birds are so special to you? And *because* you feel His presence when you see them, you look for them? And *because* God knows this, He brings them near you, or brings your attention to them, *because* of your specific memory, personality, and the joy you get from it?"

We all glanced at one another as I continued. "Now, I'm wondering if God speaks to *all* of us through whatever 'birds' we have in our own lives. Not that we all hear from God through quirky connections—but since God wants all of us to be aware of His presence, perhaps He uses ways He knows each of us would especially recognize and enjoy."

Through tears, she nodded yes.

And that's why I decided to put this story in this book.

First, I was wrong. I started this whole book saying we don't talk down about other ways people experience God—and the first time someone said something I had not experienced or heard of, I disregarded it. I had to repent.

Second, I was amazed. I was amazed that God is so loving and gracious and creative and excited for His children to know Him that He speaks to us in ways that are specific to us.

Nowadays, I don't put as many limits on what I think God can or will do to connect with His kids. All my years of knowing God personally and studying theology, history, and His interactions with His people over time have led me to this simple stance: I am not in a position to say God *can't* do something or *can't* use something. I put no limits on God. That comes with the guardrails of God's Word and God's character, of course, which we will unpack later in this chapter, but I want my stance to line up with what God *is* like—not what I feel God *should* be like.

I put no limits on God.

And everything I know of God tells me that He genuinely and fully loves us so very much, that He might even direct our gaze toward a bird that looks just like the one Grandpa pointed out to us decades ago.

The Truth About Not Feeling God

One of the most common themes I heard throughout my conversations with a thousand people was that a relationship with God can feel one-sided. Sometimes people cannot feel God or hear God. They want to feel His direction but don't know where to start. Every other close relationship in their life has an ongoing dialogue. But it's hard for this relationship to feel real when they can't feel Him, sense Him, or hear Him.

A thirty-six-year-old consultant from Tennessee said, "One of the reasons it's hard to feel connected to God is I don't always know what He wants me to do in any given situation. When it's not clear, I feel like He isn't speaking to me."

A forty-year-old nurse anesthetist from Washington said, "The hardest thing for me with God is feeling like I'm talking to myself. I don't know what He wants me to read in the Bible. I don't know what He wants me to do with my life or my boyfriend. God can't or won't speak to me."

A fourteen-year-old from Montana said, "It's hard to feel close to God when I can't see Him, and it's hard not hearing a clear response back."

A sixty-two-year-old nurse from North Carolina said, "I don't know if God hears me or will ever speak to me. Our relationship feels like a one-way street."

The verdict is in. We *want* to hear God, feel God, and know where He is leading.

But is it possible? *For all of us?*

I am going to be very honest with you: I really didn't want to talk about this in this book. I was worried that the stories I would get would be about . . . you know . . . birds. But since a big enough percentage said this was a main roadblock for them, let's bulldoze it.

There are many schools of thought about hearing from God. I'm not here to draw denominational lines or pick between your pastors. This chapter will not fully unpack all there is to say, learn, and consider about hearing or feeling Him. But for the person who is literally saying that "not feeling God's presence" or "not knowing God's direction" or "not once ever hearing from Him" is a roadblock to a real relationship with God, I want to unpack for you some simple truths. A good place to start is to uncover some things His Word *actually* says about hearing from Him . . . and to discuss what God's Word does *not* say about hearing from Him. No birds required.

When It's Not God

I have a handful of friends and heroes who have much to say about hearing God in a multitude of ways, and I want you to learn from them—so I put a list of other resources for you to dig into in the back of the book.[1] They have various perspectives to consider and beautiful ways to explore conversations with God, and perhaps in their pages you will find something that aligns best with your personality or phase of life. For the purposes of this first-steps-toward-hearing-God kind of chapter, it only seems right that you hear from me personally that a primary reason why this subject is not an area I've often written or taught about is because the message was misused on me when I was younger.

If you recall my crush who ended our nonrelationship at a bus stop, he went to a church where people expressed their love and devotion to God in so many amazing ways. As you may remember, I wanted to *be* them. One way they expressed their devotion was hearing from God and speaking on behalf of God to others, but over time it became clear to me that they did not appreciate the weight of their words. They told me (and many others) things that did not line up with God's Word or God's character at all. These "words from God" ended up being extremely ungodly, hurtful, confusing, self-seeking, and manipulative. They broke up relationships and divided our community. Some words still haunt me to this day. It painted a terrible picture of God and His church that took me years to start to heal from.

This wound of mine was a roadblock for years. I refused to listen for God, to seek His direction, for fear of not knowing the difference between His voice and my own. I also worried I would hurt others the ways others had hurt me.

I now think the enemy of our souls hopes this is the case.

He hopes you think you'll never hear God. He hopes you think hearing from God is crazy. He hopes that when you *do* hear God, you'll dismiss it and try to rationalize it as something else. He hopes when you feel led toward a decision, you don't think it's God leading you, and when you feel peace about a decision, you don't think that peace is from God. He hopes someone misused "hearing God's voice" against you, so you never want to hear from God yourself. He hopes someone abused the trust you put in them, so you never trust someone else's counsel again. He hopes you compare how you hear from God to how others hear from God. He hopes you don't even try. Because then maybe the enemy can stop you from having a real relationship with God.

That would be the worst-case scenario.

So.

Okay, fine. I'll write about it.

What Do I Know?

Out of all the passages in Scripture that talk about hearing from God or being led by God, there is one that we cannot skip over. Jesus speaks to His students about sheep and their relationship with their shepherd: "The sheep hear his voice. He calls his own sheep by name and leads them out. When all the sheep have been gathered, he walks on ahead of them; and they follow him because they know his voice. The sheep would not be willing to follow a stranger; they run because they do not know the voice of a stranger."[2]

And then Jesus makes it personal. He reveals that *He* is the Good Shepherd.

Jesus says, "My sheep listen to my voice; I know them, and they follow me."[3]

Another translation says, "My sheep *respond as they* hear My voice; I know them *intimately*, and they follow Me."[4]

The first thing we learn in this passage about hearing from God is that His voice comes out of relationship. Jesus calls the sheep "*My* sheep." They spend their days near Him. They are always listening to the Good Shepherd's voice. They know what it sounds like because of how much time they spend with Him.

The most important aspect to hearing God's voice is having a close relationship with Jesus.

In his simple but profound book *How to Hear God*, pastor and author Pete Greig writes, "Jesus is what God sounds like. He's literally the 'living Word of God.'"[5] If you want to hear from God, my first questions are, Do you have faith in Jesus? Have you met Jesus? Once you believe in Jesus and begin a relationship with Him, you talk to Him. You read about Him. You read God's Word and discover what He's like. You discover how He talks. You discover His rhythms and how He lived out His days. You read His Word while listening for His leading. God's voice sounds like Jesus. Learn what Jesus sounds like, and it will become easier to tell the difference between what is from God and what is not from God.

Once we put our faith in Jesus, we receive the Holy Spirit, whom Jesus refers to as the Helper and the Advocate: "The Father is sending a great Helper, the Holy Spirit, in My name to teach you everything and to remind you of all I have said to you."[6]

The Holy Spirit lives inside of us, empowers us, leads us, and helps us follow Jesus.

I love how my dear friend and hero Priscilla Shirer puts it. I've heard her say many times that when you're in a relationship with Jesus, the Holy Spirit within you starts to lead your convictions. She relates sensing His leading to traffic lights. Now you can detect the red light of conviction: *Stop.* A yellow light to ease the brakes or perhaps *slow down*. And the wind of God to press you forward: *Green light. Go.* As you continue to be close to Jesus, obey Him, and surrender to Him, it will be clearer where the Holy Spirit is guiding your convictions.[7]

Sometimes we want God to write directions in the clouds or spell out a phrase in our alphabet soup. We want to know what God is saying, but we don't live our lives close enough in relationship with Him to know what His voice sounds like. The truth is, the more intimate your relationship with Jesus, the more quickly you'll be able to detect when it's the voice of a stranger, the sound of your pride or your ego, or the voice of God. The more time you spend with God and His words, the more you'll know what He is like, and the more clearly you will be able to discern His leading. Simply put, the more time you spend with God, the more you'll know His voice.

How Do I Know If It's God or Last Night's Burrito?

How do we know if God is leading us, or if it's our own desires, or a dream we had last night that was weird, or maybe God, but also maybe what I'm sensing has nothing to do with anything at all? How can we tell the difference? Here are some simple questions that have helped me.

The more time you spend with God, the more you'll know His voice.

- Does this message line up with God's Word?
- Does it line up with God's character?
- Does it sound like Jesus?
- What's the worst-case scenario if I'm wrong?

There have been times when, out of the blue, I have felt someone impressed on my heart. They came to mind every time I would pray, and I sensed the Holy Spirit giving me a green light to reach out to them. Going through this filter, I came to realize: This impression lined up with God's Word. It lined up with God's character. These words sounded like Jesus. And the worst-case scenario if it was *not* a divine leading from God? Someone heard encouraging words from me but it was out of the blue and maybe they thought I was random and weird.

I'll take it. I've done weirder things.

So in moments like those, I have taken a step of faith and called that person.

For nudges much bigger than "Should I call this person?" I also bring what I think I'm sensing to trusted people. I don't bring it to everyone. I bring it to people who know and love God and who know and love me. Usually they are in close relationship with me and my husband. And, rest assured, they will tell me when I am wrong. They might say, "That's not it." They might say, "Not yet." They might say, "Let's keep praying on that together." Pray for God to reveal those people to you and seek them out. They don't have to be someone who has known you for a long time. Perhaps there is a kind and trusted person at your church. Perhaps you trust someone who is only a phone call away. Don't overcomplicate it. Pray for it, look for it, and be brave in pursuing godly wisdom. Seeking this out might seem like a great risk, but it's often a greater risk not to.

A Life with God

As a young girl, through the lens of all my hurt from people misusing "hearing from God," I would have told you, "I'll never hear from God." Now I have a very different answer. Were you to ask me today, "How do *you* hear God's voice?" I would tell you that I live my life *with* God's voice. I am in an ongoing, close relationship with Him. I don't just ask Him for specific directions on demand out of the blue. I have arranged my life around being *with* His voice, *in* His Word, in His presence, in taking risks in faith, in obeying God when it hasn't made sense, in knowing what He is like, and being around people who know what He is like too.

As I ask to be led by Him, the request is not random; it is in the warmth of a relationship. Like a sheep knows its shepherd, I know Him and can tell how His voice is different from the other voices in my life. I hear Him differently than I did two years ago, ten years ago, and fifteen years ago. I still haven't seen those birds. But I have felt the peace of God. I have felt the presence of God. I have felt the direction of God. And I have grown closer to God in my everyday life like never before.

If you're wondering about God speaking through dreams, visions, the subconscious realm of intuition, or an undefinable "knowing," there's certainly biblical precedent for that.[8] If you're wondering about prophecy, there is absolutely biblical precedent—as well as encouragement and guidelines—for that too.[9] Does God speak through signs and wonders? Yes.[10] Does God speak through a gentle silence, a whisper, or an impression in your heart of hearts? Yes.[11] Does God speak through the ordinary, through people, through creation, and through current culture? Very much so.[12] The Bible is filled with stories of God speaking to different people with different personalities in different situations in many different, beautiful ways.

Don't believe the lie that you have to feel, hear, or experience God the ways others have. That's a roadblock. Don't believe the lie that God does not want to speak to you, does not want to lead you, and does not want to direct your steps. That's a roadblock.

The truth? You *can* hear the voice of God. You *can* feel the presence of God. You *can* be directed by God. But first, you'll need to *know* what He is like and what His voice is like—so *arrange* your life around being with Jesus and living *with* God's voice. Then *ask* for God to speak to you and ask for His Spirit to lead you. Then *expect* it: Search for His voice in your everyday life. Listen for it; be open and available to notice things you haven't noticed or to feel leadings you haven't felt. (Think back to our chapter on distractions. The less you listen to other voices, the more available your mind and heart will be to hear the voice of God.)

And if you spend your life with His voice, make time to ask for His voice, and arrange your life in a way where you can hear and experience His voice without competing voices battling for real estate in your mind, He will lead you. Everything I know about God tells me He wants to speak to you *specifically*—based on your personality, temperament, and ongoing relationship with Him. And the specific ways He'll lead you in certain seasons? As one wise man in a vineyard once told me, *It depends.*

***Arrange* your life around being with Jesus and living *with* God's voice.**

CHAPTER 10

Expectations

"I CAN'T DO THIS PERFECTLY."

"I am not crushing it."

This was a text I sent to one of my best friends who lives in Austin, Texas.

I was feeling behind on everything. Deadlines, chores, emails, work projects, house projects, piled-up text messages, laundry piled up even higher, a dirty car, dirty hair . . . you name it. And frankly, following Jesus can at times feel like one more thing on my to-do list that I'm failing at.

When I haven't had enough time in prayer, when I haven't read God's Word as much as I want to (or haven't felt anything fresh from it), when I'm too tired to make plans with people, when I've said something I know I shouldn't have said . . . I know I am not crushing it.

"Me either," she replied.

No way.

We caught up on a video call soon after and shared about all the boxes we weren't checking and all the to-do lists that lingered over our heads. We were not the leaders, wives, or friends we wanted to be. And saying it out loud to each other and laughing together about the difficulty of it all was one of the most freeing days of my month. Then we started a club. The Not Crushing It Club. And you're invited to join it too.

After one thousand conversations, not meeting expectations was one of the standout answers I heard. And perhaps the one I felt the most deeply. I am not alone.

"I keep thinking there is a perfect way to be close to God, and I'm never doing or saying the right things," said my new retired friend in Missouri.

"I am constantly feeling like I am doing it wrong, guilt that I'm not doing it like my church says to, or how other people do it," said a woman in her thirties, a director of social media in South Carolina. "For example, I'm not listening to Christian music all the time, I'm not shouting and dancing in worship at church, I don't have dramatic expressions of my own faith, I don't have a crazy faith story to tell." (We will talk more about how we don't all have to worship God the same way in part 3. *Get excited.*)

"My biggest hurdle is my own expectations of how much I have to get accomplished and want to get accomplished so I can prove to God how much I love Him," confessed a dental hygienist in her forties in Colorado.

Here is a question: Where did we get this idea that we have to be crushing it all the time?

And where did we get these ideas of what "crushing it" is supposed to look like?

Where did this standard come from? Who set the bar?

A friend sent me a video on social media of a woman working

out at the gym with her kid alongside her, and on top of the background music was a voice narration saying something to the effect of, "You can be a perfect mom, a perfect wife, a perfect boss, a perfect friend, with a perfect bod, and a perfect state of mind. You got this, girl."

I mean, to be honest, it was so impressive. The mom was so fit and so beautiful, and the kid seemed to be having a great time! It was inspiring—and then, almost immediately, deflating. *How can she be so perfect and productive when I am over here wondering if this pile of laundry is dirty or clean?*

Sometimes I think we approach following Jesus this way. We reach for a standard of spirituality that doesn't come from God. The perfect Bible reading routine, the perfect Bible study group, the perfect Bible translation, Bible, Bible, Bible, the perfect church, the perfect church people, church, church, church, the perfect time to pray, the perfect words to say, the perfect way to journal. I'm exhausted just thinking about it. So I'll say this instead: As it turns out, God doesn't ask us to crush it. The expectations we feel to crush it do not come from God.

You might be thinking, *But wait—doesn't the Bible say we need to be perfect?*

You'd be right. It's in there: "Be perfect, therefore, as your heavenly Father is perfect."[1]

The Bible says it, right? That must be what the bar is: perfection. Perfect schedules, parenting styles, workout routines, and attendance at events. And that standard must also apply to our time with God, our Bible reading, our volunteering at church, our faith, and our spiritual habits. The bar is set at *perfect*.

If we live as if this verse sets a standard of stark and sanitized flawlessness, *of course we are exhausted.*

But the truth is better.

The word used for *perfect* in this verse does not mean

being ahead of everyone, crushing it, and killing yourself to be impressive.

The Greek word translated to *perfect* means "complete." It can also mean "mature" or "whole," and to *be* perfect, the active sense of the word, often meant to carry out, to complete, or to fulfill a goal with wholeness, oneness, and without duplicity. This word in its many tenses and forms meant *to be* complete and whole, and *to complete* wholly, continually, and in full measure.

God doesn't ask us to crush it.

I have no hate for the inspiring workout video from the ultimate boss mom. (You get it, queen.) But this verse is preaching a very different gospel. It's not saying, *Be impressive*. It's not even saying, *Be your best self*. It's saying, *Be whole and complete*.

Do you feel whole today?

Do you feel like every part of yourself is centered, grounded, and at peace?

Do you feel like you've invited God to heal and restore the broken pieces of your interior life, even if your outward circumstances have not changed?

Do you feel like you are always the same person at your core—online and offline, at church and at work, with family and with friends? Do you feel you have integrity when no one is watching *and* when everyone is watching?

God wants you to be whole, even when brokenness is around you. God wants you to be fully yourself, even when you're around people who tend to live double lives.

God wants *you* to be complete.

In the Gospel of John, Jesus said, "I have told you these things so that my joy may be in you and your joy may be complete."[2] Another translation reads, "I want you to know the delight I experience, to find ultimate satisfaction."[3] Jesus calls us to abide in Him because He wants us to experience the ultimate joy, contentment, happiness, and satisfaction *He* feels. When you connect with Him, you receive this—*in full*. The verse mirrors Matthew 5:48, when Jesus said He wants us to be complete as our Father is complete.

God wants you to be fully yourself, even when you're around people who tend to live double lives.

There is a theme. Jesus doesn't want us to be fragmented. He doesn't want us pulled in various directions, wearing multiple masks, or feeling like our priorities and personalities are inconsistent and all over the place. Jesus wants us to be with Him—and to be complete, just as His Father is.

I am letting out a *sigh of relief* right now.

You can too.

The call to be complete is not a call to crush it. It is a call to be with Jesus and to receive wholeness, completeness, and *non-fragmentedness* from God.

And there's one more thing: *Why* was Jesus telling them to be whole and complete? What question was He answering? What problem was He solving?

Here's the scene: Jesus was on a mountain with His students and followers, and He was teaching them what will later be called the Beatitudes—ways Jesus calls us to live. He is revealing how the kingdom of God is much different from the kingdom of the world and the lens many have been used to seeing the world through.

Jesus told His friends,

> You have heard that it was said, "Love your neighbor and hate your enemy." But I tell you, love your enemies and pray for those who persecute you, that you may be children of your

> Father in heaven . . . If you love those who love you, what reward will you get? Are not even the tax collectors doing that? And if you greet only your own people, what are you doing more than others? Do not even pagans do that? Be perfect, therefore, as your heavenly Father is perfect.[4]

There it is.

This is worth taking in for a minute. This is worth pausing to allow the Holy Spirit to undo some things we might have gotten wrong.

Jesus was never telling us to strive, work harder, or to crush it. He was inviting us to be complete in our interior and exterior lives, and specifically regarding how we treat other people. He was specifically pointing out an epidemic of duplicity, a widespread problem of people living double lives.

This has nothing to do with your workout routine.

Jesus was essentially saying, "Some of you love people only when it's convenient. You are kind only to people who think like you. You are patient only with people you can get something from. *But how is that loving like Me?* Those who don't even believe in God are like that. They love some people but not others. They have compassion on some people but not others. And the Pharisees, the religious elite? Sometimes they will act loving when others are watching. But when there's no audience, their love turns off. It's like a performative-compassion switch they turn off and on depending on whose attention they have."

Jesus doesn't want you to grow accustomed to the status quo of your current culture, favoring only those who help you get ahead. He doesn't want you to live a life of duplicity, showing kindness only when other people see it. He wants you to be fully [insert your name here] in every room you enter. He doesn't want you to be partial with your love. He doesn't want you to pretend to give love. If you are living a fragmented life on the outside, it's because something is fragmented on the inside. But Jesus wants *you* to be whole. He wants you to be complete.

Now that we know what Jesus meant, and how important it is to love God and love people (the greatest commandment, according to Jesus Himself),[5] is it possible then that the enemy hopes that when we read this verse, we do not feel healed, whole, and real but rather more hurried, frantic, and fragmented? *The very thing this verse speaks against?*

What would it look like to stop striving to complete every single goal—and to instead focus on completing God's goal: to love Him and love others *fully*, in every aspect of our lives? When you seek to love and enjoy God, your life, and the people in your life *completely* and with no duplicity . . . you will be steering into the skid of who you really are.

Welcome to the Club

I love the way Pastor Larry Osborne unpacks it. In his book *A Contrarian's Guide to Knowing God*, he talks about the extra hoops that the religious people of Paul's day made people jump through to be considered good followers of Christ. Jesus said people only needed to believe, but the religious elite also wanted people to "observ[e] all the dietary, ceremonial, and religious laws of the Old Testament as well as the traditions of the elders and rabbis." The religious people also made this extra hoop: circumcision. For Gentiles to follow Jesus, the Jewish people said that the Gentiles had to embody the lifestyle of the *Jews*. Note: Not the lifestyle of Jesus. But that of the Jews. But remember, Jesus had never taught such a thing. It was an extra hoop. It was a bar religious people raised. Osborne observes that our extra hoops today "are more likely to include well-defined spiritual disciplines, avoiding certain forms of entertainment, supporting a particular political agenda, and adopting a set of so-called Christian cultural values" that are more in alignment with how *Christ followers* want us to be instead of how *Christ Himself* called us to live. Osborne's own personal resolution is to keep "the bar as low as Jesus kept it."[6]

Louder for the people in the back.

Louder for the people in the front.

That's what I want to do too.

I don't want to water down the gospel one bit. And also, I don't want to add any of my own gospel to it. I don't want to attach anyone else's gospel to it either.

No extra hoops.

Friend, you don't have to crush it. You don't have to be ahead of everyone. You don't have to feel flawless. You don't have to impress anyone. What Jesus is really calling you to do may not be easier, but it will be better. He's calling you to be whole.

I hope today you can stop seeing your relationship with God as a spiritual to-do list and instead receive the gift of His to-don't list.

Don't believe the lie that you have to do more or hustle harder to earn God's love.

Don't try to fit into a man-made box of what quality time with God *must look like—or else.*

Don't compare your relationship with God to anyone else's. And don't compare your relationship with God now to what it was years ago.

Don't carry expectations that come from other people as if they are commands from God.

Don't let a religious lifestyle take your focus from a relationship with Jesus.

Don't let the enemy cause you to spiral in shame because you did not live up to a standard that humans created for you.

This is the truth:

"For it's by God's grace that you have been saved. You receive it through faith. It was not *our plan or* our effort. It is God's gift, *pure and simple.* You didn't earn it, *not one of us did,* so don't go around bragging *that you must have done something amazing.*"[7]

Today, you and I may need to unlearn some of the lies that have kept us from a real, grace-filled, intimate relationship with Jesus. And we may need to receive the gift of Jesus' to-don't list.

Instead of crushing it this week at everything the world is demanding of you, can you be obedient to what *God* is calling you to do?

Instead of being "perfect" by other people's standards this week, can you be purposeful? Can you look at your week and see all you hope to accomplish, then ask God to help you see what the top priority is? Will you surrender your expectations for the things that are not the most important?

Instead of feeling shame this week, will you find time to talk to God about what you are really feeling? Will you ask Him to lift the burden of the guilt and shame you feel? Will you ask Him to reveal Himself to you in this unique season?

Instead of going through the heaviness of unholy and unrealistic expectations all on your own and letting it spiral and manifest in different ways throughout your life, will you find a friend to "join the club" with you? For me, it was a Zoom call with a friend states away. Maybe for you it's a phone call. Maybe it's an in-person coffee or matcha date. Maybe it's going up for prayer at your church. Will you share with God and also with another person what is making you feel not enough? Remember there is healing and . . . *wait for it . . . wholeness* in the light.

The Pharisees, the religious people of Jesus' time, were *crushing* it. They followed the rules better than anyone, had better prayer schedules than anyone, and kept the Sabbath day of rest more strictly than anyone—yet they lived double lives. Eventually they chose their rules over Jesus and called to crucify Him. We want to be sure we don't become modern-day Pharisees. We don't want to be people who read the most Scripture but are really mean to others. We don't want to have perfect church attendance while also causing constant division. We don't want to be people who just quote what Jesus says. We want to live as Jesus said to live. We want to love as Jesus said to love. We want this to be real for us.

> **We don't want to be people who just quote what Jesus says. We want to live as Jesus said to live.**

Today, we might need to surrender the standard that does not come from God. That bar causes us to live more hurried, more fragmented, and less whole.

We might not be the perfect boss. The perfect child. The perfect parent with the perfect routines. But by the grace of God and with His power within us . . . we can be complete.

Today, I'm not crushing it in life. But I'm obeying God. And I'm asking God to help me love—completely. How about you?

Sincerely,

COFOUNDER OF THE NOT CRUSHING IT CLUB

Part 3

Shortcuts

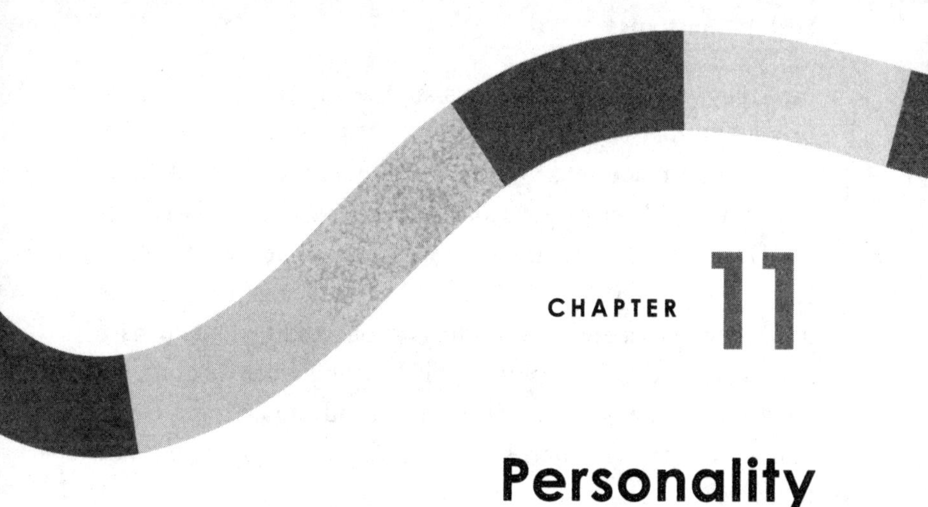

CHAPTER 11

Personality

"WHAT DO I LIKE?"

Back in the hills of Tuscany, Niccolò was not shy about all the obstacles that vineyards face. After unpacking the two questions he'd ask anyone starting a vineyard—what is your soil and what is your vision—he talked about all the roadblocks that can stand in the way of a good harvest and the best fruit. And after hearing his staggering stories of unexpected storms, flooding, droughts, pests, burst pipes, winds, weeds, mechanical issues, and human errors, we were amazed those vineyards were still standing! Not just that, but flourishing!

One of the friends we'd traveled with asked him, "How did you know how to overcome the obstacles? How did you learn everything from scratch?"

"We didn't learn everything from scratch," Niccolò said. "We've read many books. We've spent many hours and days with other people who have already done this. We heard their ideas, how they've overcome problems, and we try many of the same principles from other experts."

That all made sense to me. *Learn from the experts! Do* they *have a book with ten chapters and ten steps? Asking for a friend.*

He continued, "But then we had to fall in love with *our* soil. Know everything about it. Know all of its details. Pay attention to all the weather and surroundings in the land *we* actually have. And then we decide what we apply *here* and what we don't. See what our challenges are and what our advantages are. Get to know the weather patterns over the years. And figure out how to thrive."

He then pointed to a small shed behind us and beckoned us in with a subtle nod. The rickety floor creaked as we entered the quaint, cozy room with maps covering two of the walls and books, boxes, and paintings covering the others. As he pointed to different painted portraits of their land and vintage maps of the mountains surrounding us, he said, "This is all about the land we are now standing on. We have to know more about this soil than other soils. Yes, we are inspired by others and learn all we can from them, but at some point we have to tend to our vineyard. Sometimes what they do on their soil is not helpful to us. Sometimes it makes things harder. We must fall in love with the details of our soil."

The floor stopped creaking as Guy and I simply stood in awe.

One way to face the challenges in our lives is to understand our advantages. To overcome roadblocks in our faith and in our time with God, certainly we want to learn from others who have gone before us. We want to learn how they did it! Be inspired! Try their methods! But we must be careful not to worship their methods or directly copy and paste them. What others do may not exactly apply to what we are made of. Instead, we want to fall in love with the details of *our* soil.

The long, complicated (and impossible) way to flourishing with Christ is to spend your life trying to copy someone else's life—trying to perfectly replicate something you've seen done before. But loving your own soil is the shortcut.

In this section, we're going to talk about shortcuts—the unique ways God has already designed you and set you up for success in your relationship with Him. That's how you break through the roadblocks in your relationship with God. We are going to talk about ways to know your soil, how to love your soil, and the pathways and plans for you to connect best with God and receive all He has for you. There are traits placed within you and trails paved for you to enjoy God in your unique way. And they're multifaceted, multicolored, and wonderfully unique to you.

Loving your own soil is the shortcut.

The Word of God tells us, "For we are His workmanship [His own master work, a work of art], created in Christ Jesus [reborn from above—spiritually transformed, renewed, ready to be used] for good works, which God prepared [for us] beforehand [taking paths which He set], so that we would walk in them [living the good life which He prearranged and made ready for us]."[1]

This is good news for the introverts. Perhaps you don't need to constantly exhaust yourself trying to find "community" like the extroverts do. Perhaps you need to prayerfully seek and find one or two good friends you can get real and honest with.

This is good news for extroverts. It's possible that processing the Word of God in silence, alone, for long periods of time is not helpful in feeling closer to God. Perhaps reading it alone in shorter periods of time and talking about your findings with friends is the most natural way for you to process.

This is good news for those who are social. Think of what

social events you can attend or curate or invite people to in order to honor God and love people and foster a sense of community.

This is good news for people who are creative. Imagine ways to encounter God through your unique creative bent. It may not look like something you've seen before.

This is good news for those who are spontaneous. Have you done something impromptu this month that brought you joy and helped you enjoy your life, God, and the world He has made for you? Maybe every month you should do something out of the blue, all to the glory of God.

This is good news for the planners. If you know you do best when things are planned, perhaps it would be good to take some time to plan some restful things this year—some time with friends and family, some time with just you and God enjoying something together.

Maybe you don't relate to any of these personalities. That is also good news. Consider what helps you truly rest. Consider what helps you truly come alive. Consider what gives you peace, joy, and a sense of home. These are eclectic and purposeful pathways God created within you to experience Him and enjoy all the zest of your life.

Your details are shortcuts to God.

And your details are pathways to living out your purpose.

One of the best things you can do to live the full life God has created you to live is to go on a scavenger hunt for things you enjoy and then enjoy them with God.

Scavenger Hunt for Joy

When my time in God's Word started to feel stale and routine, I knew I needed a change. I was reading it while writing messages, reading it while researching for books. And while that work was still good, holy, and fruitful, my time alone with God in His Word had started to feel boring. I was not engaging with God Himself in the way I used to. I was not feeling any closer to Him. So I wanted to find fresh ways to love reading the Word of God again. If you can relate, here are three things to try:

- Do things you love.
- Do things you loved as a kid.
- Do things other people in your life love.

I ordered a new translation of the Bible I had never read before, with a fun cover I had never seen before. Along with it I ordered . . . gel pens. Growing up I used to love my pencil case covered in stickers and filled with various markers, colored pencils, and sparkly silver, blue, and purple pens. I wanted to reignite something in me that I had lost.

When I got my new Bible, I started in the New Testament, and as I read the same stories through a new translation, with words varying ever so slightly, I was seeing details I'd once missed. It made me want to look up those stories in other translations and in other commentaries to see if I was on to something. I circled these words in glittery gold ink. I underlined passages I'd once passed by with marvelous magentas. A few years later, I'll tell you this Bible looks like a child's Bible filled with underlines and drawings in gemstones and glitter, and I love it. This new addition to my time with God revived something in me.

I also started getting used Bibles from secondhand stores, to see what the previous owner perhaps underlined or saw in the Scriptures that I'd never seen before. One Bible from the 1960s I found in an outdoor secondhand bookstore in Boston is filled with underlines, commentary, and thoughts scribbled in the margins. (For the record, in black ink, not sparkly sapphire.)

There are thoughts the previous owner wrote that have been so eye-opening to me. Other things the owner wrote I had to second-guess and double-check and found they may have been wrong about a few things. All of this stimulated my mind and helped me see these stories and scriptures in a fresh way.

Thrift stores, gel pens, multiple translations, and reading through other people's notes on Scripture may not bring your soul to life. But good news: There are pathways in you that look different from mine and can help you engage with God in a new way too.

Sometimes discovering yourself is about *re*discovering yourself. Sometimes we need to go back to the things we loved as children to engage with parts of our personalities that have been dormant. We may rediscover from our younger selves shortcuts we have forgotten about or never saw the power in.

Finally, if you can't think of any of your own bents, lean into someone else's and try doing something someone else loves. Now, you know I'm no advocate for exhausting yourself to live like someone else, but trying things that your friends love can help you see what you *do* love and *don't* love. Perhaps go to that small group with your friend. Even though you don't think it's your thing. Even though it's a pickleball small group and it makes no sense to you how it's a real sport and you're pretty sure it's only for people in their retirement era. Maybe you're right. Maybe you're wrong. Until you find your thing . . . try all the things. Ask your friends how they engage with God, and try out a bunch of those ways too. And if you don't feel you have anyone to ask, I have filled this book with stories from new friends that you can learn from! Let's keep asking. A thousand conversations and counting.

This was true for my little brother, Elijah. Years ago, after he put his faith in Jesus, I wanted to help him know Jesus more.

(If you have never read that story, you need to! It's in my book *How (Not) to Save the World*. You won't regret it! I hope you like superheroes!) But I wondered: What was the *perfect* way for him to start? What was the perfect Bible to give him? What was the perfect translation? What was the perfect study?

I could hear imaginary voices of unholy expectations getting tangled up in my head. I thought, *Well,* this *friend would tell me* this *is the best translation. I know* this *leader would not approve of* these *translations. Well, I would be too anxious if people found out I picked* this *devotional.* I am embarrassed even reading those words back!

Instead, I had to uncomplicate it. I thought about his learning style. I thought about his personality. And then I thought about how his middle name is John. And he might like that connection.

He did.

I picked a translation of the Bible I thought was best for him, and we slowly read through the gospel of John together. We would read a chapter a day and then have a phone call or Zoom call once a week to discuss. I know it's simple. And I know it isn't everyone's favorite translation and not everyone's favorite structure. But Elijah started learning about the person of Jesus for the first time in his life. He started having a palate for the Word of God, a craving for the stories of Jesus. He started wanting to know more. Over a year's time, Elijah picked out another translation he grew to love. He started going to a local church and joined a small group. Today he leads a food pantry in the heart of San Francisco and has maintained his faith through immense trials over the past few years.

Why? Because it was real for him.

It is *still* real for him.

Other people may not have approved. But my little brother now personally knows and loves Jesus. And that's enough for me.

As for me? Slowly reading the book of John through Elijah's lens, in a translation I had never read before, then verbally processing it out loud with him, helped me see new things and fall more in love with the person of Jesus too.

Dancing 'Round the Kitchen in the Refrigerator Light

One by one, my girlfriends arrived at my front door with Trader Joe's totes, workout bags (filled with snacks, don't be fooled), and playlists on their phones paused and ready for our annual girls' weekend. We don't live near one another (two of us are flights away from the two others), and we try to see each other as much as we can throughout the year, but it's never enough. So we've made a commitment to plan at least one annual weekend a year. And with this weekend lining up with the same weekend Guy was going on a trip with his guys (lowercase g), we decided this was going to be an epic sleepover at my house and in my town for a few nights. And we had all come prepared!

One of my friends brought the most amazing recipe for glorious gooey cookies (which I still think about every couple of weeks). One brought ingredients for popcorn Rice Krispies (the jury is still out on these), and one of them brought the beverages (we all have our gifts and talents). But there was something else we had all prepared.

PowerPoint presentations.

Though we have now been friends for over nineteen years, we have not lived near one another for over fifteen of those years. We were at the point in our lives where we truly couldn't comprehend what anyone's day-to-day lives or jobs were like. So we did what at one point all of our jobs had taught us to do. Make a presentation.

Before leaving town, Guy had shown me how to hook up our TV and sound system to my computer, so the presentations would be as professional as possible. *This was very serious business.* With warm, sticky cookies oozing through our fingers, we sat in my living room. Then my first friend stood to present.

One by one we shared our weekly routines, photos, snapshots, stories about coworkers, updates on family members, quirky details, successful and failed projects, ongoing work rhythms, and colorful charts if you're the one crazy friend who loves making charts (not naming names, Kasey).

One of my girlfriends showed pictures of her sweet little boy that she raises at home, and all of our eyes teared up as she said she reminds herself, "This is a temp job. Because he won't always be this age, and it won't always be exactly this way. So I remember to cherish it all." Not a dry eye in that living room. She was right. As I am writing this, her little boy is far less little, and my friend just gave birth to a beautiful baby girl. Now that she's a mom of two, the never-ending temp job has evolved again.

Another one of my friends shared in her presentation that whenever a big goal is met at work, their boss gives them a digital llama. *What?!* Iconic. She showed us photos and we were all crying again but this time crying while roaring in laughter. We gave a standing ovation at the end of every presentation, loudly cheering, "Great job at work! You're amazing!" We had never known more about one another. It was a hilarious gathering, and I highly recommend it.

One of the things that has always amazed us about our friend group is how different we all are. We chose totally different fields of work. We live in different cities and have rhythms and lifestyles that couldn't be further from one another. We've never tried to change ourselves to be more like the others. We have always been very aware of our differences. But boy, that night, those differences were on full display, and we obnoxiously celebrated them together.

I wish we all celebrated our differences more. I wish we celebrated that we are made uniquely and that our spouses, kids, coworkers, pastors, and friends are made uniquely too. I wish no unhealthy competitiveness existed among us. I wish we didn't compare our routines to other people's, or others' tastes to our own. I wish we saw how we all make our community more lively, more vibrant, and more fun. I wish we cheered for others in the unique ways they contribute too. I wish we gave out llamas for all!

We have been created uniquely to thrive. We have been created uniquely to enjoy. We have been created to be close to others who thrive and enjoy in different ways too. If I were the enemy of your soul, I would want you to see those who can spur you on as your greatest competition. I would want you to see those who can inspire you as your opponents. I would want you to see the other "presentations" people put on—maybe not at a grown-up sleepover, but maybe on social media, at work, or at church—and feel jealous, insecure, and unwilling to celebrate with them.

Instead, I want you to celebrate how God has made you *and* celebrate how God has made others.

Celebrate your wins. Celebrate other people's wins as well.

Don't expect others in your life to live like you or encounter God like you.

Instead, look for the beauty in how differently God has made all of His children, and expect that when you are living your life fully and in your purpose, it will look wonderfully different from the other people who are living fully in their purpose as well.

Now, back to #PowerPointPalooza. After our presentations, one of my friends pulled out her playlist, cranked up the volume, and unleashed music like a wave sweeping through the house. My friends and I are different in so many ways. But one thing we all have in common is the language of nostalgia (more on that in the next chapter)! Even though we were all carrying heavy things—sick family members, lost relationships, financial hardships, and uncertainty about the future—when we play songs we used to dance to almost two decades ago, we were transported to another world. We remember the first time we danced together to a song. We remember the hard times that one year brought as well. We remember how strong we are. We remember what we've survived. We are thankful for the various seasons we've lived through together. In my heart, I thank God for His goodness. I thank God for every good and hard memory that comes rushing to mind. I celebrate that though it won't always be this way, *tonight* we are singing and twirling together in my kitchen, eating terrible popcorn Rice Krispie treats (the jury is no longer out, I've decided), in the unique way I connect with my friends and in a way that I feel closer to God.

This might not be your personality at all.

That's fair.

But I hope you know the permission you have to pause and consider what brings your soul to life. Celebrate what you discover, then imagine how to engage with God and with others through the colorful particulars of who you are. Throw a bunch of things at the wall and see what sticks. You were created to enjoy your life and your life with God. When you do that, you please and glorify Him. Llamas all around.

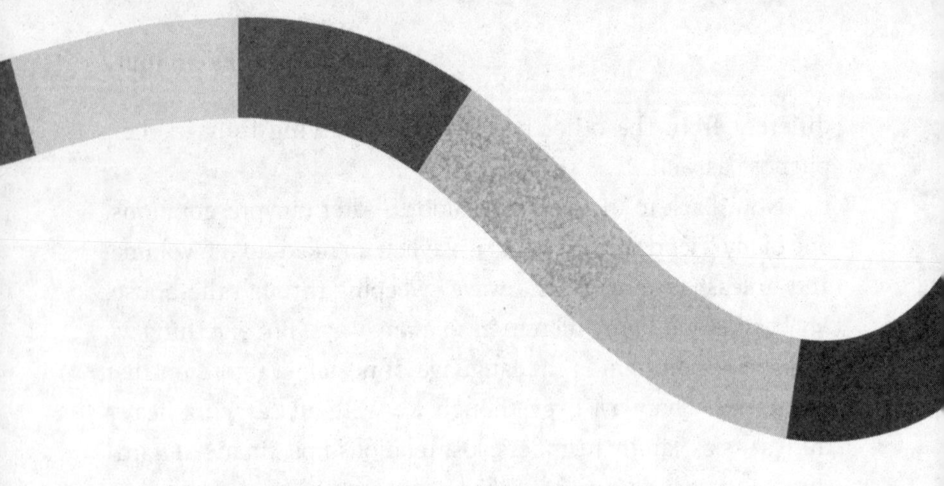

Build Your Personal Shortcut

At the end of every Shortcut chapter, I will guide you in unearthing your unique details and the specific ways you can enjoy God in your current season. To get the most out of this exercise, I encourage you to reflect on the questions at the end of each chapter and think of your honest answers.

To take it a step further, I invite you to write down your answers or the key things that stand out to you in the graphic I've included on page 219 called Your Personal Shortcut. At the end of every Shortcut chapter, go to page 219, and write key details about yourself in the chapter's corresponding box. After you've filled in all of the boxes, you will see all your shortcuts come together—to create your very own, unique, and wonderful shortcut to God. There are no wrong answers. Your Personal Shortcut likely won't look like anyone else's, and it may not look like it has in the past. That's a good thing. Be honest and write what naturally comes to mind.

Feel free to use the graphic on page 219, draw it out in your journal, or print out this graphic at hosannawong.com/shortcut.

PERSONALITY

1. What are some things that you enjoy? What's fun for you?
2. What is restful to you? What refreshes you?

Write details about your personality in Your Personal Shortcut on page 219.

CHAPTER 12

Praise-o-nality

"HOW DO I FEEL CLOSE TO GOD?"

Has anyone ever asked about your birth order—perhaps as a way to figure out what's wrong with you?

"Oh, you probably say that because you're the youngest child!"

"Oh, that's some serious oldest-child energy."

"Oh, you give off strong middle-child vibes!"

I have never known how to answer that question. I come from a mixed family, a vibrant and colorful picture of the redemption, grace, and goodness of God. God has restored what others have said could never be restored, and I love the uniqueness of my family so very much! But it's likely my family doesn't look like yours. My brother and I share both parents. My sister and I share a dad. My sister shares a mom with our other brother. He shares a dad with four other brothers. So, quite frankly, when people have asked, "Are you the oldest or are you a middle child?" I'm tempted to just answer, "*Yes!* Don't try to figure out which problems I have! *I have all the problems!* I'm first, second, and seventh!"

We laugh about it. We are far from typical.

My friends are always trying to analyze me, my birth order, and my personality traits. They send me so many personality tests. They want to know my letter combinations, my skin combinations, if I'm a fall, a purple, or if I'm Pocahontas. (Let's be honest. We all know I am Mulan, right? Let's be real. Or should I say, "Let's get down to business"?)

Truth be told, birth orders, personality tests—all of that is good and fine. But it's important to note that we can't always fit in the man-made boxes we try to put ourselves in. You cannot be perfectly pinned down or fully figured out by forty questions on Facebook. Like me, you might be in multiple places in the birth order. You might be all four seasons and all the Disney princesses. But what matters is knowing that *all of your multifaceted details are shortcuts to encountering God*.

While having a thousand conversations with new friends, I noticed some of the ways people were naturally bent to worship and encounter God. Other ways weren't as natural for some. We also see this divine diversity in Scripture. Throughout the Bible, we read of many expressions of worship and different personalities praising God in different ways—what I've decided to dub your *praise-o-nality*.

This is not like a personality test—no formulaic questions and answers to perfectly define you and stick you in a box. Not at all. I want to help you draw outside the proverbial lines. I want to help give language to some of the various, vibrant, and colorful ways you already naturally worship God. The unique makings of your personality with its natural bents and joys will help you encounter God best. Know that you will likely have multiple qualities. And there is profound beauty in recognizing and appreciating the ones you *don't* have that the people around you do.

This is not a comprehensive list, but based on the thousand conversations I had, seven unique praise-o-nalities emerged:

1. The Recreationalist (Active and Outdoorsy)
2. The Beholder of Beauty
3. The Soulfire
4. The Sacred Space Seeker
5. The Interior Expert
6. The Thoughtsmith
7. The Artist of People

As you read through the following pages, I hope you are surprised and delighted to recognize yourself and perhaps other people you know. Ask the Lord to show you His delight in how He made you and the ways that you most naturally encounter Him. He already knows and loves these things about you. Now it's your turn to recognize them and let yourself enjoy connecting with God in your own unique ways. Together let's unpack those ways, how Jesus also demonstrated them, and how Scripture has always recognized the unique aspects of how you're wonderfully wired.

1. The Recreationalist (Active and Outdoorsy)

Out of the over one thousand people I asked about how they connected with God, the Recreationalist praise-o-nality was one of the most common. Imagine my surprise, since I personally don't connect much with God this way. Already my research was humbling me. Yet this is one of my husband's bents. Guy loves going on walks as he listens to his devotionals or audiobooks, and he often takes walks to pray. And he is not alone.

A new mom in her twenties said she feels "most connected to God in nature. I feel Him and see Him in ways that are harder when I'm indoors." A server in her fifties said she feels closest to God when she can "head to a place of peace, such as the beach or a body of water, where I can escape the noise." In fact, many of my conversations were filled with stories of going to a beach, a lake, a forest, or even a neighborhood park. I was stunned. But I couldn't ignore this pattern.

Perhaps this is you. The Recreationalist often feels God is closer when they are outside in His creation or doing something active.

More than sitting in a church, it's often in the outdoors where they experience God in a way that feels like it was made for them. And it very likely was.

We see this in Scripture. We see Jesus teaching while walking by the Sea of Galilee[1] and praying in a garden.[2] In the Old Testament we see Abraham on a mountain and Jacob at a river crossing. Worshiping God while surrounded by nature is all throughout the Bible. And it's all throughout our families and friends. It's possible that you or someone you're close to has especially restful, close encounters with God in nature. Some of my closest friends do, and they are constantly inviting me to go camping with them! Personally, I don't get it. I am decidedly very *indoorsy.* But that's how they were wonderfully made (**cough* Stop inviting me! *cough**).

The Recreationalist can also be someone who feels closeness to God through physical activities. A youth director in Singapore said that when he is running or working out, "My mind is more clear and I am able to pray better, process my week better, and bring it fully to God. My mind is more at ease, and prayer time is best while my body is active."

A retired plant manager shared, "I feel closest to God when

working in the yard, thinking about a sermon, a prayer, or something my kids said. Doing something with my hands, especially outside, keeps my mind at rest yet engaged with God."

A touring musician in both North and Latin America told me in the middle of a recording studio, while leaning back in his producer's chair, "I'm a musician, so it feels like my answer should be creating and listening to music to worship God. And I do, but I actually connect with God best while I listen to the Bible and work out. That's my time. I used to feel bad about it. I used to think, *I don't know if it counts.* But it's the best time I have with Him. Like how people go to the gym with their friends? If I had a gym buddy, Jesus would be my gym buddy. I know it's weird and funny. But I've realized it counts."

It absolutely does.

One of my friends says he experiences God through both the outdoors and physical activities. He currently serves in the Army Reserve as a chaplain at the rank of major, and his service and deployments over the past fifteen years have taken him all over the world. And all over the world, he's found moments to encounter God. "Any time I'm by bodies of water—the ocean, a lake, river, creek, waterfall, you name it—I feel the serenity and peace of God. If I'm around mountains, high viewpoints looking out, they give me the awe of God. I also connect with God through walks. Walks I can usually take anywhere. I take *so many walks*. I'll usually use the entire walk as my devotional time. It's a time to calm my mind, for moments of prayer, and moments of praise and gratitude. And also road trips. Car rides alone are big for me. Whether I'm walking or driving, it's that quiet time in wide-open spaces for me. The amount of personal and internal revival I have with the Lord in those moments is pretty incredible."

I think it is too.

This does not mean that everyone who loves physical activity also loves the outdoors and vice versa, but if you love one or the other and you're looking for another way to encounter God, veer into the skid of this. Anywhere around the world. It counts.

A quick word of caution: Connecting with God in nature should better equip you to love others, not provide an escape from loving people well. Don't allow your love for activities and the outdoors to justify a life in isolation. Don't worship creation more than you worship the Creator. But absolutely tie up your shoelaces, smear on some sunscreen, and value this profound, unique way you're wired to worship.

2. The Beholder of Beauty

I had no idea how important beauty could be to some people's walks with God until I heard from one specific group of friends—painters, writers, photographers—all bonded by their love for art. We were talking about ways we experienced God that week, and my new friend who is a watercolor artist talked about the beauty of a specific flower. A friend who is a graphic designer talked about the beauty of certain paintings he'd seen that week. And a jewelry maker shared some of the most poetic prose about a small pond surrounded by flowers that she'd passed—how it reminded her of certain scriptures and pointed her toward God.

I couldn't relate. It was all beautiful to me, sure! I didn't disagree with anyone. But I could not imagine any of those things making me feel closer to God.

But for others, beauty is the most obvious and wonderful thing.

And my friends aren't the only ones.

A business owner in her thirties from Tennessee said, "Drawing, illustrating, and calligraphy" help her feel closer to God. A teacher and mom in her early forties from Arizona said she loves doodling and drawing in her coloring Bible (I didn't even know that was a thing!), and a hilarious and fun-loving freelance photographer in Texas said, "I feel closest to God when capturing moments through my camera lens. Photography is my act of worship, and it helps me focus on the beauty of creation and feel God's presence even in chaotic seasons."

One musician and writer from Upstate New York started to name specific pieces of art and music that he goes back to time and time again. "It's going to be music of a certain era for me—not exclusively, but generally music from the sixteenth century. It's weird, but it's my thing. Rembrandt's paintings that he did on sacred themes . . ."

He paused and shut his eyes as if reflecting on these special pieces.

"*The Return of the Prodigal Son*. Wow. *The Raising of Lazarus* . . . Have you seen these? Both so emotionally and spiritually moving. I know if I need to create space to encounter God, I'm going toward beauty."

I had to look them up right away. He was right. They are stunning.

Whether they're observing or creating beauty, Beholders of Beauty are wired with a unique magnet toward beautiful, created things, and this magnetic force can in turn beckon them toward the Creator God.

Jesus Himself was an artist, a master storyteller, using parables and oral stories filled with imagery, cultural references, and humor as His canvas. He unpacked complex truths in simple and memorable ways; He created beauty and was a Beholder of Beauty. He encouraged His listeners to look at the birds of the air and the flowers in the fields as examples of beauty. He wanted us to remember how much God loves us and takes care of us, even more so than the lilies and the blue jays.[3]

In Exodus 35, Moses told the Israelites that God had selected Bezalel as a master artist for the Lord. Moses said,

> [God has] filled him with the Spirit of God, with skill, ability, and know-how for making all sorts of things, to design and work in gold, silver, and bronze; to carve stones and set them; to carve wood, working in every kind of skilled craft. And he's also made him a teacher . . . He's gifted them with the know-how needed for carving, designing, weaving, and embroidering in blue, purple, and scarlet fabrics, and in fine linen. They can make anything and design anything.[4]

I love that it was God's Spirit that empowered Bazalel to create beautiful things. It was *of* God and *for* God. And beholding beauty might be your shortcut to personally encounter God as well.

A quick word of caution: Enjoy beauty, but never talk down to those who don't see beauty as you do. Never let pride or pretentiousness become a wall between you and another human being whom God loves. Let it be a shortcut to your connection, not a roadblock for others. Let it remain something holy and beautiful.

3. The Soulfire

Have you ever been in a church or worship setting where some people are outwardly expressive—lifting hands, shouting amens, or swaying to the music? Maybe you've thought, *That's a bit much.* Or, *If I did that, I'd be faking it*. It might not be your natural way to worship, but it might be a core part of theirs. While some may perform for show, that's not our concern. Remember, instead of asking, "Is this worship real for them?" we want to ask, "How can this be real for me?"

Maybe you naturally exude outward expressions of

celebration. Perhaps you sing loudly at concerts or cheer vigorously at sports games. If that's your temperament in life, it may also be your natural way of worshiping God. Others may find it excessive, but for you, a joyful, expressive environment *truly* brings you closer to Him.

In the garden of Gethsemane, Jesus Himself "fell with his face to the ground and prayed."[5] Jesus also addressed religious leaders who criticized loud, passionate worship, saying, "I tell you, if these [people] keep silent, the stones will cry out [in praise]!"[6] He welcomed bold, uninhibited celebration.

A business owner in her forties shared, "Dancing around my kitchen to praise music brings my soul to life. I used to judge people who did that—now I get it. I feel connected to God when I'm excited and joyful in His presence."

"I love loud church worship," said a retail manager in his late twenties. "I don't have a good voice, so I like churches that are a bit bigger, where the room is pretty dark, the music is loud, and the crowd is big. I feel free to sing without being judged."

A professional athlete told me about his family from Haiti and how his mom always used to play Haitian worship music on the radio. "Saturdays and Sundays were clean-the-house days, and my mom would always have the Haitian worship music playing. It would wake me up! I didn't appreciate the worship moments she was giving us at the time." But now as he trains, travels, competes around the world, and lives with an evolving schedule, he said, "One of the things I do is put on Haitian worship three or four times a week. I love the loud and lively music. I will listen to a good hour of it or more each time, and that helps me connect with God in such a personal way."

His mom and his vibrant culture and background all contribute to his unique way of worship. And he takes it on the road with him wherever he goes. We can too.

Hearing about this natural bent in some people has changed the way I look at those who are a bit more outwardly expressive—at those whose spirits are lifted in the lively and loud. Not everyone has this tendency. And if you're a Soulfire, sure—you may be constantly learning the time and place that's appropriate for outward expression. But when it's not distracting or dishonoring, I hope you know this part of you is a beautiful thing.

A quick word of caution: Worship God, not just experiences, and avoid relying on the spectacle of production for connection. Remain humble, reverent, and committed to a community of believers, noticing when it's inappropriate for certain spaces and how you can best honor and obey God. Also . . . make sure you seek out the time and space for your soul to come alive!

4. The Sacred Space Seeker

I have many friends who grew up in very traditional spaces, and observed holy days, but felt like they were being force-fed religion in a legalistic way without the grace and love of Jesus. So when they encountered Jesus in a more casual atmosphere, perhaps with more modern music or without the traditions they grew up with, they were able to experience God in a fresh way.

But I know just as many people who have had the opposite journey. They were raised in a church with loud music, bright lights, and great branding, yet they longed for something more traditional. People around them may have come off as performative or inauthentic. (Were they performing? Maybe. Or were they Soulfires? Perhaps. That's not up to us to decide.) They longed for something with more structure, with more ancient roots.

These would be the Sacred Space Seekers.

Some Sacred Space Seekers may at times feel as though Soulfires are a bit much or are outside the lines of appropriate worship. They might feel as though bright lights and loud music are counter-intuitive to a sacred space to experience God. In the same vein, Soulfires might feel as though Sacred Space Seekers are stuffy and legalistic, following rituals that can also be seen as performative in their own ways. They might feel that stained glass windows, pews, and rituals are old-school traditions that once boxed them in, traditions they've finally been freed from.

The truth? There is danger in worshiping *any* space or style more than we worship God. But the presence of God can absolutely be found in a myriad of ways and through many types of traditions. The wonderful news is that different places and spaces are available for each of us to encounter God!

For Sacred Space Seekers, traditions, holy days, and sacred spaces are deeply meaningful. For them, the rituals are the opposite of legalistic; such practices are the most real and freeing way they know to connect with God.

Abram built altars as an act of faith.[7] God commanded Moses to make "an altar of earth" for offerings.[8] Peter and John observed set prayer times.[9] Jesus went to the synagogue for Sabbath.[10] Yet He warned not to worship the ritual itself but to let it serve our worship.[11]

Sacred practices, significant milestones, and observances of holy days can mark God's presence in our lives. One father I spoke to cherished visiting his children's churches, feeling God's presence in the buildings where his loved ones worship. A couple shared how they celebrate holy days with their kids, not out of obligation but to instill faith through tradition, and use their fun celebrations as ways to unpack more from the stories of Jesus. Others spoke of feeling close to God through Communion, lighting a candle in prayer, or other rituals. Almost every time, they'd add some apology along the lines of, "I know it sounds like a religious ritual, I know it shouldn't count, but it truly makes me feel close to God." I smiled. Of course it counts. No apologies needed for the way you've been created to connect with God.

A dentist in her fifties said, "I started practicing Lent again. When I was younger, it was a religious practice we were forced to do. I hated it. After I started having my own relationship with Jesus, I realized I didn't have to do that! I was covered by Jesus' grace. I started judging people who did it. Then I had kids, and I wanted to teach them traditions without legalism. Now we practice Lent together as a family, and it's totally different for me. It's filled with so much grace. I've learned so much. I feel so much closer to God and closer to my kids. When people judge me for being too religious, I can relate. I used to be that way too. But now I am so free."

When free from legalism and unholy expectations that don't come from God, traditions, sacred spaces, holy days, and rituals are not roadblocks; they become wonderful ways to encounter God.

A quick word of caution: Seek to know God personally rather than merely through ritual. Worship must focus on God, not just tradition. Use holy practices to connect to God, not as substitutes for true connection. Remember that rituals don't save you; only Jesus saves you. But if rituals truly bring you closer to your grace-giving Savior, then that is a beautiful shortcut you should take, to the glory of God.

5. The Interior Expert

Interior Experts also seek out sacred spaces, but they don't solely find them in beautiful buildings or through sacred practices. Rather, they find them most commonly in their alone time with God. They are *solo* Sacred Space Seekers. They are lovers of stillness, quiet, and private moments with God.

I got the term *Interior Expert* from pastor and writer Eugene Peterson. He writes of how all of us "must learn how to deal with the interior of our lives and become experts in it."[12] And this is certainly true. We are called to live honestly before God, and that will take times of silence, prayer, and honest reflection. Though this may look different for each of us, we are all called to this work.

In addition, for some of us this is a natural bent that we gravitate toward. Interior Experts are not necessarily *actual experts*, as if they know all there is to know about themselves. But they are explorers of their interior lives, inner-world archaeologists bent toward digging up what's beneath the surface. They are comfortable in a quiet place alone with their thoughts. They are naturally introspective and drawn to deep reflection on how their journey, Jesus' teachings, and their inner and outer world connect. They find joy in private encounters with God. They love unseen sacred moments. Public or private, what matters to them is that it's real, meaningful, and impactful.

I'll admit it now. This is one of my praise-o-nalities, and I can feel the superiority creeping in as I want to say, "This is the *best* one!" *I repent, Lord. It's not the only way. It's one way. Got it.*

Some find introspection boring. If that's you, you're probably not an Interior Expert by nature. That's okay! Too much quiet time alone might sound like your worst nightmare. For some of us, it's a sacred space.

In Matthew 26, a woman poured expensive perfume onto Jesus' head, and His followers thought it was a waste. But it was her way of adoring Jesus. There was a personal story and sacrifice attached to the act that they couldn't have known. That didn't concern her. An Interior Expert has a deeply personal and intimate relationship with Jesus that they are alright with no one else understanding. It likely includes inside jokes, memories, and thoughts that at times feel more sacred in secret. Some of my friends can relate.

A mom in her thirties said, "There's nothing like being alone, on my knees, with no distractions—just me and God. I feel deeply in these moments, and my faith comes alive. Being alone, I can feel my feelings, and feel God." A college athlete said he has journaled daily since childhood: "It brings me closer to God as I reflect on what He's done and reread my journey."

One trait Interior Experts might share is a love of nostalgia. Playing certain music brings them back to a sacred place. Recounting certain memories re-engages their faith. I know this has been true for me. Listening to certain songs from certain times in my life, then replaying the goodness of God in prayer, is one of the ways I feel closest to Him. This was true for me and my girlfriends as we danced around my kitchen to some of our favorite songs. We found something holy in the nostalgia. And I was shocked to learn that many of those I interviewed could relate.

A dear friend of mine who is an executive pastor, writer, and musician told me about a practice he does once a year. "On Christmas morning, I get up at four a.m.," he said. "It's absolutely silent in our house. I make a pot of tea, then I light a few candles. I turn on the Christmas lights on the tree, and I start a fire in the fireplace because I'm a San Diegan and any temperature below sixty will give me severe hypothermia. And then I sit quietly and I listen to Christmas music. Not 'Grandma Got Run Over by a Reindeer.' I actually listen to choral worship music. Specifically, I listen to the choir of Merton College as they sing these beautiful hymns in Latin that remind me of the timeless and eternal nature of God. They force me to slow down—to sit in the quiet, connect with God, and marvel at the fact that He chose to be God with us. How much of Scripture is 'Don't forget'? 'Don't forget My faithfulness, what I've done, who I am.' And I thought, *I've got to be better at remembering. I've got to slow down my pace and remember.*"

He turned toward his computer and said, "This is my Christmas playlist." He hit Play. The harmonies began to fill the room.

"Then I read Luke 2, which talks about Jesus' birth," he continued, "and I just sit. In the presence of God. And I thank God for everything He's done in my life. And then I think of all the hard stuff that's happened this year. And then I thank God for being 'God with us'—God with me—in the middle of even the hardest times. And I remember. And I just quietly worship Him."

His story of his solo sacred space has stuck with me.

If you're an Interior Expert, lean in. Find personal, engaging ways to pray, meditate, and reflect. Make space for sacred moments. Enjoy your inside jokes with God. Dial back the clock and crank up the nostalgia. Worship in a unique, personal, and quirky way. Perhaps while surrounded by choral hymns in Latin with the Christmas lights twinkling above the steam of your tea.

When I learned others enjoy God this way, I thought, *Maybe I'm not crazy. Maybe I'm not a hermit. Maybe solitude, reflection, and nostalgia are simply ways I encounter God.*

Jesus did too. He sought lonely places to be replenished.[13] After feeding thousands, He led His disciples to a quiet place for rest.[14] He spent forty days alone in prayer and fasting, emerging stronger.[15] Jesus knew which battles to fight because He first fought to spend time alone with God.

Personally, I often need absolute quiet, no devices, and no distractions, even in other aspects of my life. As I write this chapter, my phone is in another room until I meet my writing goals for the day. When I spend time with God, my phone is also in another room. For some, this might seem legalistic, but for me, it's necessary, helpful, and holy.

My husband is different. He can read, pray, answer work texts, check his email when someone says they sent him something, and immediately return to his time with God without missing a beat. That would completely derail me. But if I told him, "If you don't wake up super early, read your Bible immediately, and leave your phone in another room, you're not truly encountering God," I know he'd just smile and chuckle, kiss me on the forehead, make coffee (before praying?! *What?!*), and go on his walk. What a Recreationalist. And what a free child of God who has already uncomplicated it.

We are made differently. But we are both made to encounter God.

A quick word of caution: Don't love your alone time more than you love God. True interior surrender should make you more loving and more gracious in the exteriors of your life. Purposefully pair your personal faith with community engagement or service to guard against worshiping your sacred space more than you worship God. Don't judge those who struggle with longer periods of quiet or alone time. But if that's how you enjoy God the most, pull out those nostalgic playlists, go to your solo spaces, and in the name of Jesus, enjoy God to the fullest!

6. The Thoughtsmith

This one isn't about being the smartest among your friends. (If it were, I'd be counted out for sure.) It's about feeling closest to God when you learn something new about Him—such as when a familiar passage suddenly has a fresh meaning. When you've read and heard a story about Jesus for decades, only to discover something new about it, it brings your soul to life in ways you can't express. You feel Him closer. You want to know more. That's what being a Thoughtsmith is like. This is another one of my top three praise-o-nalities, so I'll try not to be biased about this one.

If worship feels too feelings-based without sound doctrine, it can frustrate you—not because you're a pious academic judging others but because you crave understanding. Perhaps this is why I asked my crush in high school and all his family members so many questions. I didn't want to just go through the motions. And I wasn't asking *why* we did certain things to be annoying. I knew understanding would truly help it become more real for me. For Thoughtsmiths, when your mind isn't engaged, worship can feel empty. If your mind *does* understand it, you might be the most engaged person in the room.

Jesus sought out biblical understanding as well. As a teenager, He went out of His way to read and study Scripture.[16] It might go without saying that Jesus already had a spiritual connection with God, yet even He still craved greater understanding, curious to know all there was to know about God. Thoughtsmiths are naturally curious and can sometimes be found researching history, theology, systems, science, and biblical studies to understand Jesus in a deeper way. When a light bulb goes off in their mind, something illuminates their soul.

A biology product lead in her early forties said, "My best time with God is quiet time outside. As a biology textbook editor, I encounter Him in the details of life—you know, cellular and ecosystem processes." I love the way she said, "*You know.*" I chuckled. I *don't* know what she means, but she does—and that's how she experiences her Creator. Amazing.

A caterer in her thirties said, "I enjoy listening to theology and apologetics from people I trust. 'Nerding out,' I guess, on biblical principles. When I learn something new, I get so happy I feel like I'm praising God inside of me."

I can relate. I once struggled with Jesus' invitation to abide in Him; it felt important, but I was not sure how to do it practically. So I researched. I spoke with vineyard workers, lab scientists, and over a thousand people about how this concept applied to their lives. And because of that, I began to see how John 15—abiding and connecting with God—relates to real lives in a way I never had before. And it changed my relationship with God for forever. Writing this book became an external outpouring of an internal transformation. I leaned into my praise-o-nality and embraced how I'm wired—and through that, I encountered God more deeply. You are holding the fruits of my steering into that skid.

A quick word of caution: Be sure to be faithful in obeying God, not just in learning a lot about God. Being closer to God should make you more humble, so as you discover more about Him, resist pride, unnecessarily correcting others, or loving controversy and debate more than people and their hearts. As you pursue learning more about God, it should also empower you to see the world the way He does and help you love people better. Don't just love information. Let God's love inform how you live. And may your random findings and all the fun facts be a sacred fire that fuels your faith.

7. The Artist of People

This list is not structured according to order of importance, but I did want to end the praise-o-nality discussion by sharing a story I heard in the hills of Tuscany, back at the family-owned winery that started this whole thing. One day during lunch on their land, we sat at a large table overlooking one of the daughters' vineyards, sharing stories and hearty laughs and so many savory cheeses with the family and the other visitors. At one point I saw the owner, Annibale, get up and stand looking out over one of his three vineyards. I walked over to him and we stood together in silence taking it all in. Then I asked, "What are your daughters like?"

He grinned from ear to ear.

In broken English and through a wide smile, he described each one. One daughter was an artist; he talked of her paintings and sculptures, and how she was one of the best artists in the family, maybe in the whole area! Another daughter he described as an artist of administration. He said she was so smart and could run the business part of their vineyards better than anyone. Then he paused. He turned to look straight at me as he described his final daughter. A story of her growing up. A vivid memory he held close to his heart. A thing she had said that made him laugh. Then he said, "She's not an artist of paint. She's an artist of people. Like you. You're an artist of people."

This final temperament is for those of us who connect with God best through other people—our conversations and relationships with them.

Jesus Himself was a people person, stopping to help the sick, to make friends, and constantly inviting people to eat with Him (or inviting Himself over to other people's houses).[17] Jesus had so many friends, and so many people enjoyed His company. We have to assume He was probably a good hang.

We were all created for community, but some of us have a natural bent toward it.

A woman in her early sixties said, "Teaching others through a women's Bible study, being a part of women's leadership Bible study, time with friends and family, and being open to invite or receive an invitation from anyone in my path—that's how I connect with God best." A thirty-nine-year-old man who had just started a business told me, "Talking about God with friends is my new favorite thing." There's something about conversations about God that helps us come alive in a fresh way.

If you're an Artist of People and the Bible has started to feel stale and lifeless, a good idea might be to start talking through Scripture in community. Start reading the stories of the Bible with a friend or a group of friends. Let your conversations and shared insights give you a fresh perspective of Jesus.

This praise-o-nality can also include a natural bent toward hospitality and serving others. For many, hosting and serving other people is a genuine way to encounter God. An office admin in his late forties said that when he volunteers at church or in the community, he "truly feels closer to God and grows to understand God and His love more." He added, "I know it's not supposed to be about what you do, and I don't think it's about what I do—but doing things with my hands for God and doing things for others makes me feel closer to God. I feel most myself that way. It just feels right. It feels like worship." It is. If you can relate, loving, serving, and caring for others might be your shortcut to God.

A quick word of caution: True worship serves God, not personal validation. True worship is not about people loving you; it's about you loving God and others. While you serve people, make sure it's done out of love and not ego. As you show up for the needs of many, be sure to prioritize your loved ones and not neglect family in the name of helping others. Serving must come from a place of love and surrender, not personal fulfillment or a need to prove yourself. And when action does come out of that genuine love—when it's truly connecting you to God and to people—that soup kitchen you're serving at, that Super Bowl party you're hosting, and that honest conversation you're having over hot wings and fries can be one of the holiest places in the world.

Free to Worship

These different ways to encounter God are not meant to box you in; they're meant to set you free. They are meant to show you how people all over the world have natural bents that are also reflected in Scripture and might be reflected in your life and your community as well. They are to show you that there are some ways you might worship God that might be totally different from others in your life, and the best way for all of us to encounter God is to be fully ourselves before Him. The long way around to enjoying God is to try to be like someone else. *Being who you are is the shortcut.* And that shortcut is likely wildly colorful and possibly lined with light bulb moments. It also could be full of hikes in hoodies, stained glass windows, or loud and quiet moments alike.

Some things to keep in mind:

1. You likely will relate to more than one of these praise-o-nalities.
2. You might have different bents in different seasons. Throughout your life, you might be all of them at different times and encounter God in each of these ways at some point.
3. If you're not sure which praise-o-nality sounds most like you, try a few things out. Experiment to see what makes you feel most like yourself while also feeling most connected to God.
4. Remember this is not an extensive or exhaustive list. But I hope it can be a great place to start!

One more thing to be cautious of: It can be helpful to know the ways we are wired, but we never want our wiring to stop us from being challenged or stretched in other areas of our faith. Just because you don't have a natural bent toward being an Interior Expert does not mean that God does not want to have one-on-one alone time with you or that you don't need to reflect on what's going on within you and bring it to God.

Just because you aren't a natural Soulfire or a natural Sacred Space Seeker doesn't mean God might not call you to take a step of faith in different expressions of worship. It can be helpful and holy to stretch ourselves a little beyond our comfort zones of faith. And it's also good to recognize the beauty of the ways we are wired so that when we are spiritually and emotionally exhausted and unsure of how to connect, we can steer into our skids and allow others to steer into theirs.

You may have noticed a theme running through my conversations: *"I know it's weird." "This is weird and funny." "I didn't know if it counts." "Does this count?"* Hearing these phrases so frequently for months on end made me more certain than ever that we badly need permission slips from God to be ourselves (who He made) and encounter Him in our real lives (what He wants). The enemy of our souls doesn't want us to enjoy God for real—so he hopes we'll think faith must look one specific way *or else*. He hopes we don't enjoy Jesus as our gym buddy. That we don't find Him while listening to Haitian worship music, lighting candles, singly loudly, singing softly, reflecting, nerding out, or hosting dinner parties. Why? Because the enemy knows what we need to know: that we were all wonderfully created to enjoy God in unique ways. The weird and funny stuff? It counts. And it was made on purpose.

As we lean into our unique temperaments and acknowledge the bents of others, do you know what I believe will happen? We will actually encounter God *more*. We will more regularly notice the ways we're already naturally encountering Him. We will take back the joy that legalism once stole from us. We will feel less shame. We will be less judgmental. We will be more gracious. We will free up others to encounter God more deeply in their own ways. And each of us will experience God . . . *for real*.

This especially goes for my outdoorsy friends. I love you. But please stop inviting me to camp.

PRAISE-O-NALITY

1. What are your top three praise-o-nalities in your season right now?
2. What are specific things you love about each of those?

Write out your praise-o-nalit(ies) in Your Personal Shortcut on page 219.

CHAPTER 13

Personal Structure (Trellis)

"HOW CAN I BEST RECEIVE FROM GOD IN THIS SEASON?"

How do we actually do this?

We now know we don't want to compare our relationship with God to anyone else's relationship with God. We now know we want to engage with God with our real personalities. So now, as our honest selves, where do we begin?

I am almost jumping out of my chair because of how excited I am to tell you this. I learned something new a few years ago that changed my everyday life with God. While Jesus was on earth, His students (the disciples) had many questions about how to live. (See? We're not crazy.) And one of the answers Jesus gave them was this:

"Abide in Me, and I will abide in you."[1]

We waded into this passage a few chapters ago, but now we're going to swim in it.

Abide may not be a word we use much in our everyday lives, outside of the context of Scripture, but what the word means is actually very familiar to us. To abide means to stay, to remain, to dwell. Other definitions say to sit down, remain sitting, be, trust, stay over.

In fact, another Bible translation uses those words: "Live in me. Make your home in me just as I do in you."[2]

Jesus was basically saying, "Make Me your home. Rest with Me as your shelter. Live with Me as your protection. Trust. Sit. Get comfortable. Get cozy. Let down your guard, take off your shoes, and put on your favorite hoodie. Live here. Stay over."

Then Jesus moved on from a picture of a home and started painting a picture of branches that need nutrients to live. He told us how those branches would get what they needed only when they *rested*, *remained*, *got comfortable*, *and lived off* the vine.

I mentioned I've been studying vineyards for years—since even before Niccolò and Annibale blew my mind. Here are some of my favorite findings. *Thoughtsmith moments for days. My nerd alert is on.*

Jesus said, "A branch cannot bear fruit if it is disconnected from the vine, and neither will you if you are not connected to Me. I am the vine, and you are the branches. If you abide in Me and I in you, you will bear great fruit. Without Me, you will accomplish nothing."[3]

Jesus wanted those who followed Him then—and those of us who follow Him now—to know this: True connection with God does not happen by doing. It happens by *being*. It does not happen by working. It happens by *with-ing*. (Note to my editor to ask Webster himself if we can make *with-ing* a word. You have his personal number, right?)

Simply put, when we are with Jesus, spending time with Jesus, and remaining in His presence, just as branches get nutrients from a vine, we get all we need from God.

When you are abiding—remaining and dwelling with Jesus—you are in a position to receive all that God has for you. Abiding, at the end of the day, is not about what you can do *for* God. It's about being in a position to receive *from* God. And for many of us, we aren't always in a place to receive. But there is a way . . .

They Didn't Tell Me This in Church

I have known this verse on abiding for most of my life. I have even taught on it in churches! But then years ago, something happened. My world shook. My husband, Guy, and I went through a season of immense loss—physical, financial, and relational. The people we thought would stay, didn't. The people we thought would defend us, didn't. I started down a spiral of guilt and shame, replaying scenarios over and over in my mind of what I should have done better. I started to lose who I was. I felt distant from God. I felt distant from people. I felt distant from myself. And I knew the answer to receive all God had for me was to first *abide* . . . but I could not figure out *how.*

Do I just sit in my backyard and try to force my mind to rest? (Forcing myself to rest doesn't sound right . . . right?)

Do I just drive around in my car and say, "Okay, God—I abide"? (Cue Carrie Underwood's "Jesus Take the Wheel.")

Do I just sit at my kitchen counter with my eyes closed, trying to will myself to remain?

This sounds good and spiritual, but it started to feel fake and unrealistic, because I couldn't will myself into peace or joy or closeness to God. Once my life had derailed, "abiding" no longer seemed like a simple answer. I needed to know how. I needed steps. I needed something practical to do to get me out of the feeling of being stuck.

I called up a good friend from Portland who has worked in wine and vineyards in Oregon, California, and New Zealand. She didn't grow up in church, so I knew she wouldn't give me a churchy answer. I could count on her to be gritty and practical—and also, in that moment, *agricultural*.

As soon as she picked up, I started firing off questions:

"How do branches get connected to a vine?

"How do they stay connected through storms?

"How do branches get reconnected if they become disconnected?

"Is a connection to the vine really all branches need to survive?"

She laughed. Then said she was going to plug in her phone because she could tell this would take a while.

I get that. Charge it up.

Then she said, "Well, technically yes. All the branches need to live is to be connected to the vine. But what really makes this possible is a trellis. Branches need a structure. They need supports that hold them up and help them stay connected to the vine."

She went on to say that a trellis keeps branches from getting tangled. It gives them more air circulation, the right amount of shade, and an even amount of sunlight. And it ensures the branches are fully engaging with the vine and receiving all the nutrients they need to grow and flourish to their full potential.

So of course my next question was, "What's a trellis?"

You've probably seen a trellis or two in your daily life. Here are a few examples.

These are all different kinds of structures, made of either wood or metal, that support the branches, the flowers, and the growth of a vine, plant, or tree. You might have seen one of these as an entryway to a garden, wedding, or park. Or if you're really bougie, maybe you have one in your own backyard. (I mean, I don't have one, but if you're highly favored and fancy like that, God bless you! Also . . . please tithe at your local church!)

If you look for trellises, you will start seeing them everywhere. Ever since she told me about them, I feel like I see them every day. If you see one and think of me, take a picture and tag me online. I'd love to see it. We may just start a trellis-spotting revolution.

But at the time of this conversation with my friend, needing a structure was a new thought to me. Thank goodness for phone chargers, because I had more questions.

"But *to live*, I thought all that branches need is to be connected to the vine."

"Yes," she said. "All branches need is to be connected to the vine . . ."

Then she paused, and after a beat, added, "But without a trellis, without a structure, the branches will live their lives constantly weighed down. They will be carrying weight they weren't meant to carry. They will fight an uphill battle they don't have to fight. Eventually they can break apart from themselves and from the vine."

Exhale.

Does anyone feel weighed down today?

Perhaps you feel weighed down by your never-ending to-do list. Weighed down by the disappointment that your life didn't turn out the way you had hoped. Weighed down by the expectations of people. Weighed down by your own expectations. Perhaps you feel weighed down by physical and mental fatigue. So much is going on around you and in you, it's hard to put it all into words.

Does anyone feel weighed down today?

For those of us who feel weighed down, there is a way to come alive again. There is a way to be connected to God and to *stay* connected to God. And as it turns out, the answer for many of us is a structure.

Your Personalized Trellis

When Jesus' students watched Him live and tried to live like Him, they would have seen firsthand what the structure of His life looked like—what He did throughout the day, the week, the month. These rhythms made up Jesus' lifestyle, the structure of His life. And as Jesus called His disciples to follow Him,[4] He was inviting them to put their faith in Him, obey Him, and also literally *follow* His lifestyle.

I'm sure you're familiar with this concept. If you want to shoot hoops as good as Steph Curry, you study how he spends his weeks, how he practices shooting, how he builds muscle, and how he rests. You want to observe and understand the lifestyle of the greatest shooter of all time.

If you're an artist and you want to be better at your craft—better at songwriting, woodworking, graphic design, dancing, or another form of art—it makes sense to learn from the habits and techniques of others who are accomplished in those fields. You want a similar life structure to those who did it best.

I adamantly agree with Eugene Peterson when he wrote, "Jesus is the best look we have at what it means to be human—*really* human."[5] And if we want to follow the lifestyle, habits, and posture of anyone who has cultivated a life that remained in God, we want to follow His example—the greatest human example of all time.

Jesus' life structure included daily, weekly, and monthly rhythms, such as prayer, rest, and celebration, all of which we will unpack more fully in the next chapter. But it's important to note that Jesus' rhythms weren't simply for the sake of routine. These rhythms were ways to best connect with God and to best receive from God. Jesus, by living example, was teaching His students *how*. He was answering their questions of how to live. He wanted to teach us as well. Jesus' life structure involved a set of habits that kept Him *abiding*—at home with God. From Jesus we can discover a personal trellis that puts us in the best position to flourish.

Releasing the Weights

Whether you are just starting your relationship with God or have been following Him for a long time, this can't be overstated:

Once you put your faith in Jesus, that's all you need to be saved.

Period. That's it.

But at the same time, it's possible that while you know you have eternal life, you might not feel like you're living a full life *today*. Today, you might not feel yourself flourishing. Today, you might be fighting uphill battles you don't need to fight.

Perhaps you just recently put your faith in Jesus, and now it's time to build a structure to help carry the weights you weren't meant to carry. Maybe it's time to pray on and plan your own personal trellis and to take your next step in starting some new rhythms. I will help you start this.

Perhaps you have known, loved, and served God for a long time. Maybe you have had a structure—you've prayed, rested, and served enough to teach a master class on it! But lately you have felt weighed down as well. You've stopped receiving life from the scriptures you're reading or stopped receiving joy from your time in prayer. Perhaps you've started to wonder: *Is this real for me? Is this all there is? Did my faith peak? Is there some unresolved sin in my life?*

To briefly answer that last question: *Maybe there is!* There may be something God is calling you to surrender to Him. And we won't skip past that. We can't.

But first, I don't want you to automatically assume something is wrong with your faith. It might be that you are just growing more fruit.

What?

Let me say it again so guilt and shame can get pulled out like the weeds they are.

If you are comparing your relationship with God to what it was in the past, I want to remind you that you don't have the same life you once had. You might be in a season of bearing *more* fruit; there may be more growth, more impact, and more life change. You might have new responsibilities. You might have new relationships. You might be dealing with new tensions. You may be in a new leadership position. A new position in your family. A new role at work. The heavy weights you're feeling might not all be bad weights. You might be weighed down because of how much fruit has been growing in and through your life.

You might simply need a *new structure.*

The structure that could hold you up ten years ago might not be strong enough to hold you up now.

You will not be able to keep growing if you hold on to the structure that held you up before.

Stop living weighed down by guilt and shame because of all the good fruit in your life.

It's time to look at your real life—today.

Your relationship with God does not have to look like anyone else's relationship with God. And your relationship with God does not have to look like it once did.

Your season is not a roadblock.

Your season is your shortcut.

Take a deep breath.

No matter where you are in your faith journey today, it might just be time for a new structure.

Your relationship with God does not have to look like anyone else's relationship with God.

The Point Is to Receive

Before we go further, I want you to know the structure is not the point. The point is to be in a relationship with Jesus Himself, the Source of life. This book is not going to teach you how to curate the perfect, pristine structure of sacred practices. That's how we get in danger of living out our faith like it's a performance, like it's a list of boxes to check, like it's a way to win a flashy medal for being "The Most Spiritual and Having the Holiest Habits." We must be careful. We must not raise a generation of Jesus followers who care more about their spiritual practices than personal closeness to Jesus Himself. That is how the enemy gains victory over us—by convincing us to worship the structure more than the One the structure connects us to. Let me be clear: There is no salvation in the structure. There is no life in the structure. Salvation, life, and power are derived only from the Source, Jesus Christ Himself. The best thing the structure can do is help you not live weighed down to the point where you are not receiving from the Vine and not flourishing in your life.

One of my heroes is Watchman Nee, an evangelist, missionary, and leader who helped establish churches in China in the early to mid-1900s before he was persecuted for his faith and died in prison in 1972. His writings have had some of the greatest impact on my faith and my unique relationship with Jesus. While in prison, Nee wrote of the progression of an authentic believer's life as first *sitting*, then *walking*, and finally, *standing*. He emphasized the need to sit with Jesus first. But some of us flip that order.

Nee warns, "Too many of us are caught *acting* as Christians. The life of many Christians today is largely a pretense. They live a 'spiritual' life, talk a 'spiritual' language, adopt 'spiritual' attitudes, but they are doing the whole thing themselves. It is the effort involved that should reveal to them that something is wrong."[6]

Almost a century later, I echo his sentiments. Too often we focus on what we think a Jesus follower is supposed to *do* before we focus on being *with* Jesus Himself. When we try to live out the *exterior* expressions of faith we assume Christ followers *should* live out—especially before we sit with Christ, know Christ, and allow Him to transform the *interiors* of our lives—we will be in danger of living out a performative and powerless kind of faith. We are trying to *stand strong* and *walk well*, but we have neglected to start with a posture of *sitting* with Jesus.

Too often we focus on what we think a Jesus follower is supposed to *do* before we focus on being *with* Jesus Himself.

But make no mistake: The invitation from Jesus is first and foremost to be *with* Him—to *abide* with Him and to sink into the cozy couch of closeness with Him.

You can create a structure that helps you make yourself at home with Jesus today.

If you're thinking, *I don't want another to-do list*—good. That's not what this is. We'll create a personal structure for this particular season, one that works for your personality, praise-o-nality, and present schedule, and you'll have all the permission in the world to pivot.

Perhaps your personalized trellis for this season will not be a set of rhythms perfectly planned for the whole year. What would be helpful for *you* in this season? Maybe it will be a structure for a week. Perhaps it will be for a month. Maybe for a semester at school, or your sports season, or for a six-week work project you're in the middle of right now and you know your schedule is going to change after that. *Great.* Let's plan a structure for *this* current season.

This is not about living heavier. This is about living lighter.

A trellis—an intentional, personal structure—helps you receive from God.

You were never meant to live so weighed down.

You were always meant to receive all that God has for you.

And how can you be in the best position to receive it? For that, turn the page.

PERSONAL STRUCTURE (TRELLIS)

1. How would you describe the season you are in right now?
2. What sort of structure would be helpful for your season? One week, one month, a two-month stretch, a school semester? What length of time do you want to plan a structure for? What would serve your current season?

Write out details about your current season and your personal structure in Your Personal Shortcut on page 219.

In the next chapter, I will show you an example of what it looks like to plan out your own personal structure, your own trellis, in your real life.

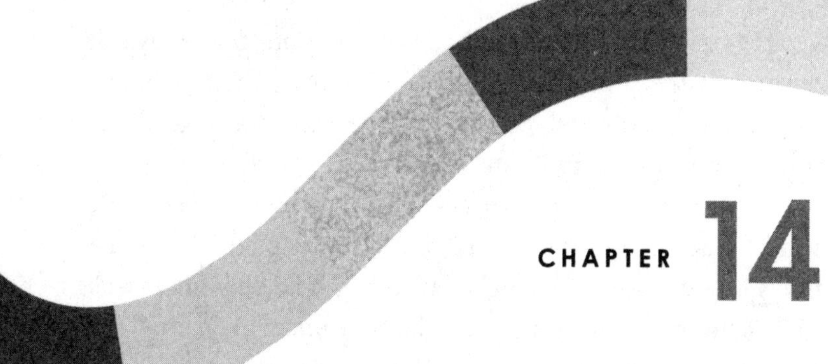

CHAPTER 14

Practical Supports (Rhythms)

"HOW DO I DO THIS PRACTICALLY?"

The sky was a swirl of raspberry and orange sorbet as the sun set over Tuscany. Since we were in Italy, I suppose it was more like gelato. Our time with Niccolò, Annibale, and his gracious family was coming to an end, and we were all standing on top of a small hill watching the sun sink lower and lower. I turned to Niccolò to use my remaining time to ask about trellises. *Obviously.*

First, I shared with him what my friend had said to me on the phone about how a trellis helps carry weights the branches weren't meant to carry, and he loved that picture. He smiled wryly like a proud papa looking over at the vineyards he tends to, and in his strong Italian accent said, "Of course those are mostly different as well." *Of course he said that!* I thought to myself. *He's committed to being very unhelpful!* (Just kidding.)

He continued, "It all depends on location, the vineyard's position to the sun, what fruit it will produce, and how much. You have to build what's best for that specific grape to get all the sunlight and all the nutrients it needs."

I commented how downright pretty I thought trellises were, and he laughed out loud. "Sometimes it's very pretty, and sometimes it's very ugly." We laughed together. If he only knew what trellises represented to me, he'd know I understood that sentiment in more ways than one. "It isn't about being pretty," he continued. "It's just about [being in] the best position, for health and growth and fruit and harvest."

He spoke more about the best practical functions of the trellis—improving air circulation for the branches, placing them in the best position for sunlight, and forming a framework of support for branches to grow upward, while also helping them carry the weight of their fruit.

Though the sun continued to settle in, new thoughts were dawning on me.

I used to think, *What do I need to* do *to connect with God?* But as the sun went to sleep in Tuscany, I realized I wanted to know how I could cultivate a life that *remains* close to God, that *stays* in the best posture to receive from God.

Jesus shows us how.

The rhythms we learn from the lifestyle of Jesus are similar to the practical supports in the structure of a trellis. This is what we will unpack as simply as possible in this chapter.

Remember, it's not about your trellis looking pretty or polished or presentable for the world to see. It's about being in the best position to receive all God has for *you*. This is for your health, your growth, and your fruit. Also, remember, there is no power in the structure. So with grace, and freedom, and without any ounce of legalism, let's look at the lifestyle of the best human who ever lived, and see how we can best learn from His example, His rhythms, and follow Him.

None of these rhythms will be fully comprehensive; many wonderful books and studies have already been written on each. But see this section as more of a dictionary than a commentary. I want to give you some shortcuts for the times when you are not sure where to start, how to connect, or how to keep growing. Like a good trellis, what I'm offering are some practical supports for your personal structure to help you when it comes to *untangling*, *engaging*, and *closeness*. With some support, you can receive all you need from the one true Vine.

Untangling

Without a trellis, branches can still grow—but they'll often grow in the wrong directions. They can become tangled with themselves, pinched and suffocating, losing airflow and failing to receive the nutrition they need from the vine. This can also be true for us. We, too, need a Great Untangling. Here's how Jesus did it . . .

Untangling Through Real Conversations with God (Prayer, Silence, Solitude)

I often call my silent alone time "untangling the noodles." Maybe it's because I'm Chinese and I often think in Asian food metaphors. But it's true; my thoughts, emotions, worries, to-do lists, and grocery lists often feel so tangled up. When I sit in my backyard with no electronics and no other noise besides the hummingbirds fluttering near my fig tree or the sounds of cars gliding by, or when I take a walk around the block with either nothing in my earbuds or simple instrumental music echoing between my ears, I am able to be alone with thoughts. I am able to think, feel, and invite God into what I am truly carrying, where I am hurting, and what I am hoping for.

Yes, it may take true intentionality in our day and age to make this happen, to put our phones away and leave the to-do list on the counter with boxes still unchecked in order to have alone time with God (remember the distraction roadblock?)—but this fight is worth it. Real, one-on-one conversations with the One who knows you the best and loves you the most will bring your soul back to life.

I find it hard to hear God's voice when my mind is a crowded room of other voices and noises. Silence and solitude open the door for real conversations with God—for God to have conversations with me, for His words and His peace to have room and space, and for me to honestly speak back.

Prayer may look different for each of us depending on our personalities, praise-o-nalities, and our specific seasons. Today, this could look like praying while walking. At another time, this could look like praying in the morning, before going to bed, or on the drive home from dropping off the kids. This could look like prayers of lament, prayers of thanksgiving, or prayers of petition, asking God to powerfully intervene in a situation in your life. This could look like liturgical prayers, prayers through Scripture, silent prayers in your heart as you wash your dishes and inhale the scent of lemon dish soap, or prayers of gratitude as you stand in line for street tacos, breathing in the holy aroma of carne asada. Praise God.

This is what many call "practicing the presence of God." We learned this in chapter five, from my new friend who is a mom of four. This looks like inviting God into everything you do, even in the most ordinary tasks—talking to Him, being interruptible, and being open to His leading all throughout your work-meetings-and-house-chores-and-errands-upon-errands days.

Jesus Himself lived out this rhythm—He lived in constant conversation with God. He talked to His Father in many different ways, at different times of the day. We see Him going to a mountainside and spending the night praying to God,[1] waking up early to go to a solitary place with God,[2] praying prayers of thanksgiving,[3] praying prayers of lament and grief,[4] praying for miracles,[5] and praying for others.[6] He invites us to live similarly. He does not demand we pray the same exact way, at the same exact time of day for our whole lives. But He does ask us to follow Him, and if we truly do, we will follow a rhythm of finding and making time to talk to our Creator.

As you practice the presence of God, you will discover the knots within your heart and mind untangling. As you have real conversations with God throughout your real life, it will feel like coming up for air. Like the supports of a trellis, the structure will help you not feel suffocated, twisted up, or weighed down. Instead, you will be strengthened—put in the best position to receive from God and find yourself at home with Him.

Untangling Through Real Rest

Throughout the Gospels we never see Jesus rushed, in a hurry, or in His head. Instead, we see a rested, untangled Savior. Jesus prioritized going out of His way to spend alone time with God.[7] He cared about His disciples getting rest.[8] And we see that even Jesus, after a long day of teaching thousands, "in the rear of the boat, was sleeping on a pillow."[9] Rest was a rhythm of Jesus and one He invites us to follow. Just like branches without a trellis, we carry weights we are not meant to carry when we don't get real rest. We get tangled up in the expectations of others and the unrealistic expectations we put on ourselves. We start to think we must do more or produce more or hustle harder to prove our value. A rhythm of rest will help us. It's a support that is meant to keep us from suffocating and straining to flourish.

Jesus actively engaged in Sabbath rest—one day a week of stopping, enjoying, and delighting in God—but He didn't always observe it the same way. The religious people hated that. They had very strict rules around the specific days and the specific ways the Sabbath was to be carried out. They worshiped their structures more than they worshiped the Source of life. They were tangled up in the wrong priorities. They were complicating the way to God, though Jesus came to uncomplicate it.

Jesus came to uncomplicate it.

What would it look like to follow the pace of the Prince of Peace? What would it look like to spend one day a week untangling through rest? What would it look like to not work or produce for twenty-four hours and instead *stop* and *enjoy* and *delight* in God and the life He's given you?

The rhythm of weekly rest is not just a rhythm of sleeping (though that is good, and literally what your body and soul need). Rather, this rhythm also means *engaging* in restful activities. Your body and soul also need that. What would bring your body physical, mental, and emotional rest? It's not about *not* doing; it's about what will truly untangle the productivity within you and give you a fresh breath. Your soul needs air circulation. Your feelings need to stretch. Rest is part of a Great Untangling. Think back to your personality and praise-o-nality. Perhaps engaging in rest for you is being active or being outdoors. Perhaps it is a day of fun with friends. Perhaps it is seeking out a sacred space, a garden, a gallery, or a concert in the park.

A software engineer in her forties from California said she loves "escaping the hustle and bustle of life and heading to the beach for rest. Maybe I'll surf, maybe I'll swim, maybe I'll read fiction."

A mortgage loan officer in his fifties from New York said he loves "walking, running, and finding alone time with God through fitness and just being in the outdoors."

A woman in her late twenties on staff at a church in Singapore referenced *both* untangling rhythms—conversations with God *and* engaging in rest. I asked, "What would you tell someone who doesn't know how to start spending time with God?"

She responded, "I would ask, 'How do you spend time with your best friend?'" She then talked about her ongoing conversations with God, both casual and deep, sometimes silly and sometimes somber, sometimes filled with many words and sometimes none at all. She talked about leisurely rest as well as lively activities, planned times together and spontaneous meet-ups. She talked about the comfort of that kind of relationship and the freedom and fun of connecting with God in this way. I loved that.

This beautiful untangling will look different for each of us. But real conversations with God and real rest are practical and powerful supports. They help us receive from Jesus, the Vine—the Source of real life.

Engaging

In a vineyard, a trellis helps the grapevine's branches receive all the nutrients they need by placing them in the best position for engagement with the vine. Throughout our lives, we also want to flourish; we want to be in the best position to grow into who we truly are and to live the full lives we've been created to live. Jesus shows us how . . .

Engaging in God's Word

It will be difficult to receive from God if you don't personally know what He says and what He's like. Engaging in God's Word is one of the most important supports in your trellis, as it helps you forge a genuine relationship with God—getting to know Him for real and receiving all He has for you. But it's important to note this doesn't simply mean *reading* the Bible. Some of us may have believed that reading the Bible was a requirement for a good Christ follower. Maybe we believed that if we weren't reading it early enough, long enough, or regularly enough, then we were doing something wrong. But how often have we met people who *do* read their Bible every single day—reading it early and reading it for hours—yet are not very kind people? They are not peaceful. They are not joyful. Is it possible we have made reading the Bible a structure to be worshiped instead of a structure that helps us connect with the Source of life?

The notion that reading the Bible is important is not incorrect, just incomplete. The goal was never just to read the Bible but to *know*, *understand*, and *engage* with what it says—to know God and get closer to Him. We don't want to be people who are good at solely knowing *about* God without truly knowing God Himself. We don't want to be good at quoting Scripture but bad at living it out.

The goal is not to read the most Scripture. The goal is to know the Author.

If reading the Bible early and for long periods of time is not helping you engage with God, the answer is not to wake up even earlier, read even longer, or tape open your eyes. Instead, you may need to engage with God's Word in a new, fresh way. Remember your personality and your praise-o-nality. Think about reading it slowly, perhaps one chapter at a time. (Like my brother and me, you can start in John, if you want.) In your car before heading to work or after work. You could listen to the Word, perhaps while at the gym. Consider finding or creating a community to discuss Scripture with, or using fancy tools like . . . gel pens. You have permission from God to engage in your own way.

The goal is not to read the most Scripture. The goal is to know the Author.

Jesus Himself had a rhythm of going out of His way to be in the temple to read what was written of the Word of God at that time.[10] If Jesus Christ, the Savior of the world, intentionally engaged with God's Word, how much more do we need to do the same? Jesus' example demonstrates that the effort will be worth it. In fact, it will become a vital support in your personal trellis.

Engaging in Worship

Worship will look different for each of us, depending on our temperaments and praise-o-nalities—but at the end of the day, worship is a posture of surrendering to God, obeying Him, and giving Him glory. Here's what I heard in my conversations with new friends:

"I say thank you at random times of the day and always thank Him for specific things. I listen to praise music. I jump and sing and dance to worship music in my room," said a seventeen-year-old student from Atlanta.

A talented touring artist from Arizona said, "Whenever I take a risk for God, a step of faith, I feel Him closest. It's my most surrendered form of worship. Every risky yes has been worship. And as I obey, tithe, serve, and forgive, it's all a surrendered 'I love You.'"

These are great examples of worship. Worship can certainly look like singing and dancing in your room, like our young friend from Atlanta. But the first moments where we witness worship in the Bible do not involve music, instruments, or song lyrics at all. We read of Abel offering up sacrifices to God,[11] then Abraham obeying God by saying yes and surrendering his son.[12] The first story is when we first *see* worship, and the latter is when we first see the word *worship* mentioned in God's Word. And both times, the worship is not through singing. It's through obedience. It's through putting God's desires above anyone else's. It's through sacrifice and humility. Here we are introduced to *worship*.

The Hebrew word for *worship* in Genesis 22 means to bow down.[13]

And in Romans, the apostle Paul urged us to *live a life* of bowing down. He said, "I urge you to offer your bodies as a living and holy sacrifice *to God*, a sacred offering that brings Him pleasure; this is your reasonable, essential worship."[14]

Be a *living* sacrifice. Be obedience, surrender, and humility—embodied. Living and walking and talking in your everyday life—*worship*.

Practically speaking, here are just a couple of ways you can worship God:

Look for ways to obey God every day.

Live with a posture of surrendering to Him every day.

Sing songs of worship, pray prayers of worship, give generously as an act of worship, and live each day with a spirit of continuous thanksgiving.

Singing is not the only form of worship, but it certainly is a powerful way to worship. For me personally, when I engage in speaking and singing the truth about God, it drowns out all the other voices in my head. The noodles start to untangle. My praise becomes louder than my problems. My worship becomes louder than my worries. When I know I am too tangled up in my head, I lift my hands and lift my voice and declare the goodness of God.

Jesus lived a life of obedience and worship. We see Him

worshiping God through His words ("I praise you, Father, Lord of heaven and earth"[15]) and through His life's walk ("He humbled himself by becoming obedient to the point of death, even death on a cross"[16]). As we set out to follow Jesus, we are invited to do the same. With our words and our walks, may we be living and active embodiments of worship.

Closeness

If branches don't remain attached to the vine, they won't have what they need to flourish. A trellis with good supports facilitates this vital connection.

God created us *for* community and has called us to be *in* community—but simply being *around* people was never the goal. When we mistake this as our goal, we might find ourselves in a room full of people, at a grocery store or concert, or even at church . . . and still feel lonely. We might hear people say, "Get in community," and not know what that means or what a healthy version of that looks like. This is all fair. So instead of *community*, I like to use the word *closeness*. God created us for closeness with Him and closeness with others. Not to just be near them physically but to find a deeper level of connection. Getting real about what you are going through, and celebrating what God has already done and is doing, will bring you closer to God and closer to others.

God created us for closeness with Him and closeness with others.

Closeness Through Celebrating

Jesus was a master at celebrating. He called out the wins, He encouraged and celebrated His friends, and He planned and prepared for holy celebrations. While the religious elite of Jesus' day practiced many sacred rhythms, we have no record of them celebrating. We have no stories of them having fun. So I wonder: If we never live like Jesus—whose spirit of celebration breathed life into His sacred rhythms—will we, too, develop a pretentious and lifeless faith?

Dallas Willard cautions us that "we dishonor God as much by fearing and avoiding pleasure as we do by dependence upon it or living for it."[17] So often we are taught to abstain from pleasure, and certainly we should not indulge in pleasures that separate us from God. But it is also important that we *do* indulge in pleasures that bring us closer to God.

Eugene Peterson encourages us to follow Jesus' lifestyle: "Christ's way of life is a holy attack on everything that leaks the brightness out of our lives or detracts from the promised joy of our faith. It demolishes anything that promises liberation but, in fact, imprisons us in boredom. Following him evokes a life pursued heartily and meaningfully."[18]

What would it look like to join Jesus in the holy practice of *party*? Not partying in a way to feel numb but in a way to celebrate God and others and to feel fully alive. As you put time aside to celebrate and are vocally thankful to others and to God, you will execute a holy attack on the heaviness that holds you back, and you will unlock a lightness and joy. One fruit of this practice will be not taking yourself too seriously. Instead, you will *seriously* enjoy the life God has given you.

Closeness Through Getting Real

Getting real is one of the most important supports in your structure, keeping you truly close to and receiving from God. Others might call this *confession*. If you don't get real about what is hidden inside of you, it will weigh on you, keeping you from living the full life God intended for you. You can start feeling suffocated—losing your spiritual air circulation and hitting a spiritual roadblock. And yet this shortcut can free you.

Psalm 32 says,

> Then I let it all out;
> I said, "I'll come clean about my failures to God."
> Suddenly the pressure was gone—
> my guilt dissolved,
> my sin disappeared.[19]

If you have done something you're not proud of, confess it. Let it all out and allow the pressure to be released. The apostle John reminded us that "if we admit our sins . . . He'll forgive our sins and purge us of all wrongdoing."[20]

We've already talked about how shame is a roadblock. But Jesus is the ultimate shortcut. When you put your faith in Him, He forgives you and makes you clean. You can stop living in shame that Jesus already came to set you free from. Getting real removes the roadblock of shame between you and God and makes it possible for you to fully receive His forgiveness and grace.

Stop living in shame that Jesus already came to set you free from.

And Jesus demonstrated this. The night before He died on the cross for our sins, He "bowed with his face to the ground, praying, 'My Father! If it is possible, let this cup of suffering be taken away from me. Yet I want your will to be done, not mine.'"[21]

Jesus did not have sins to confess as we do, but confessing sin is not the only way to get real with God. Confession can be an honest conversation with God about what we are really feeling and going through.

If we don't get real with God about what's burdening our hearts, our relationship with Him will suffer and grow stale, and our interactions with God and others will become performative. However, there's a better way: Honest self-auditing and transparency with God and trusted individuals is a shortcut to deepening our connection with Him and others.

Get real with God. Get real with another trusted person.

We are told in the Word of God to make this our "common practice: Confess your sins to each other and pray for each other so that you can live together whole and healed."[22]

This is what I discovered with my cofounder of the Not Crushing It Club. Once we shared the truth of what we were going through without shaming each other, we experienced a freedom we had longed for.

And on days when we *did* have a win, when there *was* an open door, when we *did* feel peace in a chaotic season, we called each other as well. We engaged in the holy practice of party.

Celebration plus confession equals authentic closeness. They are practical and purposeful supports in your personalized structure that lift the weights of shame, complacency, and loneliness off you. Closeness does not happen overnight, and it does not happen by accident. It takes effort and intentionality. And sure, it can be physically exhausting at times. But I promise you it's even more exhausting to live a hidden life. Closeness is the key to flourishing.

Closeness Through Great Hangs

The hang is holy. Jesus showed us that. Jesus traveled with His friends and disciples and "relaxed with them"[23] in the countryside "where they could enjoy one another's company."[24] He had meals with tax collectors and thieves[25] (sinners who needed grace), as well as the religious people of the day[26] (more sinners who needed grace). He was constantly at dinner parties, eating and drinking with everyone.[27] Jesus lived a life of closeness to people, and He calls us to do the same.

Since you were created to be in community, a part of yourself will lie dormant if you live your life in isolation. Through all my hundreds of conversations with new friends, I found a theme of longing for, seeking out, and then eventually finding a new closeness to God through a safe and fun community.

A thirty-eight-year-old preschool teacher in Alabama said, "Church or small group weekly, at least one of them, has been a game changer in my life. No guilt if I can't do both, but always grateful and more at ease when I can do one. I love worshiping with other people and connecting with them and their stories."

A fifteen-year-old in Kentucky said, "I love talking to other people about their experiences and sharing testimonies. That's how I feel the closest to God and people. That's sometimes at church, but sometimes at school or at swimming."

Pastor and author John Ortberg writes of the fun and the friendships cultivated through serving, saying, "It is almost impossible to serve without creating a greater sense of intimacy and community."[28]

It actually surprised me to hear "serving" as a way to feel closer to God and to others in many of my conversations with people. I heard it time and time again. This is from my friend who is retired in Indiana: "I've had a new wind in my sails and faith while serving in different areas of the church—like our food pantry, on our greeting team, or serving communion. I'm connecting with people more and connecting with God more."

A part of yourself will lie dormant if you live your life in isolation.

A fifty-three-year-old accountant in Washington told me his

favorite way to connect with God was "through outreach. When I see others come to Christ because of the example we are living out as a community, and the ways we are serving our cities, I know this is what God intended, for us to be living examples of Jesus, and I've never seen the church like this before, and I am so proud to be a part of it."

The fruit of serving is simple. Serving helps us be more like Jesus, with the posture of Jesus—not thinking lower or higher of ourselves than we ought to—and opens up doors to be closer to people and to God. If your natural praise-o-nality is an Artist of People, this might come easily for you. If it's not, it might be a new support to add to your trellis—a new rhythm for you to try so you may, in turn, receive something new from God and His people.

Closeness looks different for everyone. And that's a good thing. When we shed our expectations of what it *should* look like, then take a step of faith into a safe and authentic community, we'll find that our lives are not more polished but rather healthier, stronger, and filled with more fun and faith than ever before.

The Lifestyle of Jesus

We don't have to live weighed down, tangled up, or torn apart. Jesus modeled a lifestyle—a structure of rhythms that kept Him close to God and His purpose—and we can follow this lifestyle as well. Just like a support structure that makes it simpler for branches to stay connected to the vine, the rhythms of untangling, engaging, and closeness can be integrated into your life's personal structure—all in your own unique way.

Look at your month, or your week, or whatever structure you chose in the last chapter. A calendar covered with its vertical and horizontal lines tends to look a lot like a trellis. It could be helpful to write out and plan for when you will follow these rhythms of Jesus in your life, in this season. It does not need to be intense. It can be simple. And it doesn't need to look like anyone else's structure. But the important thing is to look at your actual life and to pause, pray on, and start to plan how you will follow Jesus, follow His rhythms, and cultivate a lifestyle of receiving all God has for you.

We've looked at just a few rhythms, but certainly there are many more. In his book *The Spirit of the Disciplines*, Dallas Willard lists fifteen. In her *Spiritual Disciplines Handbook*, Adele Ahlberg Calhoun explores over seventy-five. Even then, none of these lists are exhaustive, and the best way to follow Jesus fully is to read about His life in God's Word yourself. But these supports in your personal trellis are a great place to start.

In fact, for the purposes of this book, I've chosen to call these practices *rhythms* of Jesus and *supports* in your trellis instead of disciplines because I want us to fully grasp, even in our terminology, that these are not rigid rules we must flawlessly follow in order to be saved. We are saved by the grace of God through putting our faith in Jesus. Period. But these supports, these rhythms, help us stay at home in Him. They are made *for* us. They help us receive. They help us flourish. These supports are our shortcuts.

My prayer is that you would never be tempted to worship the supports themselves, or worship the structure of your trellis, but that you would live out the rhythms of Jesus in your life, in your current season, and will feel closer to the Source of life than you ever have before.

It doesn't need to be complicated.

The road is narrow, but it's not supposed to be confusing.

May we uncomplicate it.

Hanging out with our Best Friend, serving, singing, sitting in silence, and untangling all the noodles—together.

PRACTICAL SUPPORTS (RHYTHMS)

1. What are ways you can untangle?
2. What are ways you can engage?
3. What are ways you can practice closeness?

Write out details about your practical supports and the rhythms you want to live out in Your Personal Shortcut on page 219.

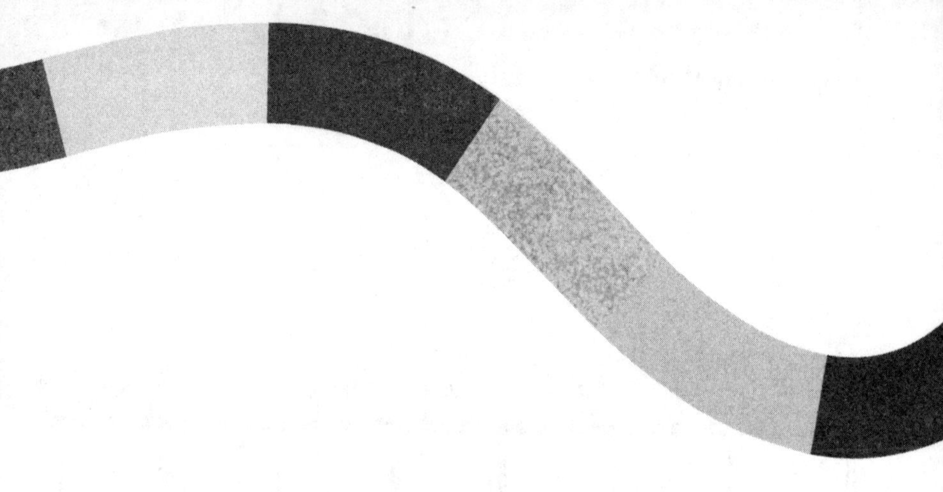

Build Your Personal Trellis

With all you discovered in chapters 13 and 14, what would it look like to create your personal structure (trellis) with your practical supports (rhythms)? Your structure might be for a year, a quarter, or a week. In the following pages, I've included graphics for you if you wanted to plan out a month.

You will find one of the trellis graphics from chapter 13 with days of the week lining the top. With seven squares vertically, and four horizontally, it looks a lot like a month's calendar.

Think of the rhythms you want to start, and sprinkle and schedule them throughout your trellis—your month. I've included an example for you as well. Think about how you will untangle, engage, and practice closeness this month.

Fill out the trellis calendar in this book, or print out your own at hosannawong.com/shortcut.

Sun.	Mon.	Tues.	Wed.	Thurs.	Fri.	Sat.
Church (worship)			← (Conversations with God) Morning prayer + reading through John (God's Word) →		Coffee with Patriece (holy hang, celebration, confession)	no work - sleep in - hike with hubs - basketball game at night (real rest)
Church (worship) Lunch with family (holy hang)	Start new devotional (God's Word) Evening prayer, silence + solitude (Conversations with God)			date night with hubs! (holy hang - celebration)	Retreat weekend! (worship + holy hangs) Devo + Reading through John (God's Word)	
Walk with Jacqui before flight back (holy hang) No work - reading (real rest)	← Morning prayer (Conversations with God)	Dinner with Carolina (Celebration)	Devo + Starting Acts (God's Word) →	Small group (holy hang)	Brunch with Natalie + Bethany (holy hang) Day off - beach day (real rest)	Quiet morning (real rest + prayer) Dinner with Lori + crew (holy hang + celebration)
Church (worship) Lunch with Max, Avery and Kit (holy hang)	Reading through Acts (God's Word)	evening walk to worship and pray (worship + conversations with God)		Small group (holy hang)	Allison, Lindsay + Kasey coming over for dinner (holy hang) ← Reading Acts (God's Word) →	sleep in - boxing class - roadtrip with hubs! (real rest)

Sun.	Mon.	Tues.	Wed.	Thurs.	Fri.	Sat.

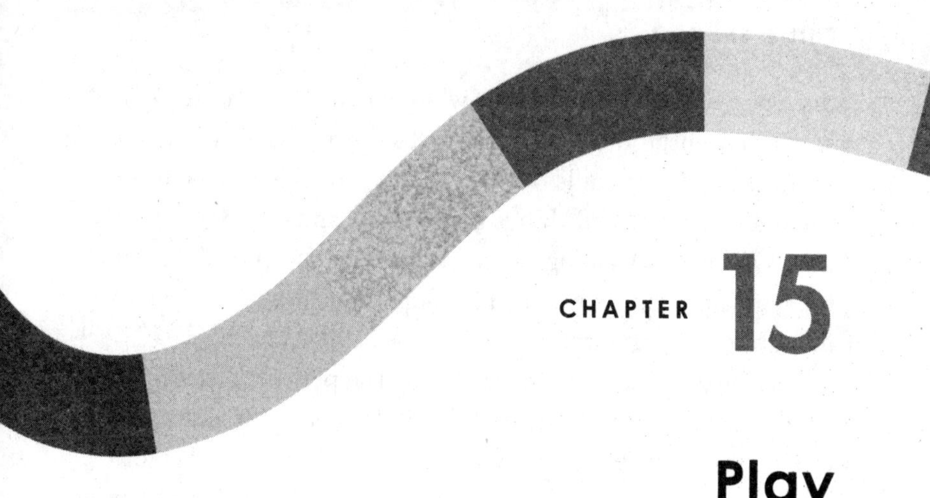

CHAPTER 15

Play

"WHAT IF I DON'T LIKE STRUCTURE?"

What if you have a personal structure with all sorts of rhythms, a trellis with all types of practical supports, but you simply *hate* structure? Or what if you *love* structure or *want* structure, but in this season of your life—when everything feels out of control, up in the air, or out of your hands—structure is just literally impossible? Maybe you are thinking, *The last two chapters were just fine for someone else, but structure and supports are not realistic for me right now.*

I have one of the most freeing messages to share with you.

After years of unearthing what vines and vineyards can teach us about abiding, I found myself looking around a stark, white lab in Paso Robles, California, with an associate winemaker. She wore a coat resembling Bill Nye the Science Guy's and was surrounded by different wine samples being tested around the room. If you knew a student in your chemistry class in school who loved beakers, thermometers, scales, and multiple shades of dry-erase markers painted on a white board . . . then this room would have been their grown-up self's dream. Better yet, it was set in the romantic hills of wine country. And that winemaker was the epitome of all things cool, nerdy, and beautiful, all in one. We love a ravishing, research queen! I didn't ask her, but she would probably have liked my Superman/Princess Leia look in high school. Just saying.

She had worked in wine for years. The perfect person to get some practical answers from. I asked her about the need for a trellis. "Is there any chance a vine could survive without a trellis? Is there any way a branch could stay connected to the vine, then flourish with fruits, even without such a supportive structure?"

She smiled. "Yes, there's a way. It's called *head trained in goblet*."

Ooh. The plot thickens.

Goblet is a French word pronounced "goo-ba-lay." This type of vine care is named after a goblet—think valiant knights and esteemed ladies and their glamorous golden chalices making toasts at their festivals and feasts. That cuplike shape is where this method gets its name.

One single wooden stick or stem is placed at the base of the vine. This is far less intricate than a trellis structure, but it also requires much more attention and care from the one tending the vine.

She talked about the need to constantly check the roots, the leaves, and the cadence of the consistent pruning. She talked about the vinedresser's hand pulling leaves that were covering certain fruits and the personal attention each vine requires when it has only this minimal structure. She called it "constant canopy management." Without a typical trellis structure, she said, the one tending the vine would need to have their own personal kind of structure—a hyperawareness of the health of the vine, its branches, and its fruit. "It's a lot of work, but it's possible," she said. "You don't *need* a trellis to help you. If you're hyperaware, you can do without it."

To summarize in my own words: This is more freestyle.

In fact, Niccolò's answer to this same question in Tuscany confirmed what she'd said. I asked him, "How will you know if you need a trellis or if you can head-train in goblet?" First, he replied with his now-famous nonanswer: "Depends." Which I still sort of hated at that time and had not yet realized the beauty of. He talked about different soils, different regions, and whether certain mechanisms were available. Some places, he explained, were literally not capable of having an extensive trellis. "What if I could have either?" I asked. "Which should I choose?"

He laughed and waved his hands and said something in Italian I couldn't make out. Then he said, "Use anything else before trying *in goblet*. Anything else at all. Any trellis. Any structure. Does not need to be fancy. It's okay if it's ugly. Anything to help. Otherwise it is very hard and very time-consuming. Any trellis will help make this better and more enjoyable and make better fruit."

He continued, "Goblet is helpful in extreme climates or extreme seasons, when it's the only option—but most of the time you have so many other options."

I could take this metaphor so much further, but for the sake of real-life application, let's stop here.

Permission to Freestyle

A trellis—*any* kind of structure at all—is better than training in goblet. It's better to have systems that water; schedules to nourish and prune; supports that hold up the branches and keep them untangled, engaged, and connected to the vine; and so much more. In your life, it's good to have some sort of structure. It's good to have some version of a regular set of rhythms. Your structure doesn't have to be fancy, and it doesn't have to be as intricate as yours has been in other seasons (or as intricate as other people's with different soils). It doesn't have to produce fruit that looks like others' fruit. Your structure doesn't have to be daily. It can be weekly or monthly. But try to find a structure. And then, when it's literally impossible to build a structure because of your season? Where you are in your life right now: *in goblet*. Freestyle. It may take more intentionality, but if you can be personally attentive to every aspect of your spiritual life, you can still produce good fruit.

Now, looking at Jesus, our perfect human and our example to learn from, He seemed to do both. He *had* rhythms but was not rigid *when* He lived them out. There was a structure to His life—there were things He committed to do to keep Himself connected to God, but they were not always at the same time of day, in the same type of way, with the same people.

Jesus prayed in the early morning.[1]

Maybe you were taught that the morning was the only time to pray or perhaps the holiest. Plot twist:

Jesus prayed in the evening.[2]

Jesus prayed in the middle of the day.[3]

For some of you, those three verses are all you needed from this book to be set free from any unrealistic expectations. For Jesus, there was a structure, and there was a freestyle as well. Ideally for me and my personality, there's a bit of both too. There's absolutely a trellis in my current season and a bit of growth happening in goblet. There's a structure that's helping me be intentional, and there's freedom to freestyle.

I'll never forget one conversation I had with a woman from Tijuana, Mexico. She said when her daughter who was in her thirties unexpectedly died, the grief was so immense she couldn't function for months. She thought she had to pray a certain way to talk to God, so she stopped talking to Him altogether. "Then I changed two things," she told me through tears. "One, I stopped trying to pray pretty. I started praying ugly. Yelling. Crying. Telling God I'm mad. I'm hurt. It's unfair. I'm broken. I'd go days without talking to Him. And then I'd pray unpretty again. And praying unpretty prayers brought me closer to God. Telling the truth brought me closer to God. And closer to my family. And now I lead a women's small group where it's the most raw and unpretty things we are sharing, and it's the most real friendships I've ever had. It has started to heal something in me and in us."

After we wiped away our tears, I asked, "What was the second thing you changed?"

"Oh. I started praying at night."

I laughed while patting down my now-very-dewy face. "What do you mean?" I asked. It sounded so simple.

"Yeah," she said. "I always thought I had to pray in the morning, but that doesn't work for me anymore. My whole life is different now. I don't care what people think anymore. I stopped trying to live like I did before my daughter died. Now I pray at night. If people say that's no good, who cares?"

Amen.

What can you do if your life has changed and your previous structure isn't working anymore?

What if you *could* have structure but you *hate* structure?

Switch up your structure! Have a much looser one. One that is specific to the season you're in, that involves what you like and works with your actual schedule.

Or see this season as your goblet season. Flexible. A freestyle.

Or see it as a little bit of both.

But the good news is that no matter what your life looks like right now, and no matter why you had to change up your plan for connecting with God, a personalized plan is always available for you to stay close to Him. Your relationship with God was never supposed to be a rigid formula you tried to fit into. It's always been real friendship you're invited into. And when you're walking through a dark valley, or when your life feels out of control, or when the plan you've grown used to goes out the window, God is still close to you and longs to be in a real relationship with you. Don't hide from God because you feel like you can't stick to a certain formula. Perhaps now is the season of freestyle. And that can be a beautiful thing.

Your relationship with God was never supposed to be a rigid formula you tried to fit into. It's always been real friendship you're invited into.

Pray and Play

Eugene Peterson talks of Sabbath, a weekly day of rest, as a day where "we pray and we play." I love this posture toward a day of rest, and it's a phrase I have integrated into my daily life. Beyond one weekly day of rest, I want to live in this posture every day, for when we aim to live a life praying and playing, "we become more ourselves, not less, living more in the image of God, living more truly in touch with family, friends, self, and the world."[4]

What would it look like for you and me to live a life of praying and playing?

As I mentioned earlier, you have permission to throw a bunch of things at the wall and see what sticks. Try going on walks while talking to God. Try getting a new translation of the Bible and starting somewhere different. Try volunteering at a new place at church. Try doing something in faith this week you've never done before. Try praying for an extended time once a week. Try asking a group of friends to start a book club with you. Try something different and see how it connects you to God.

Pray: Invite God into your everyday life.

And *play*: Do things with God that bring you joy.

Pray, play, in goblet. (It doesn't *look* like it rhymes, but when you say it out loud, it most certainly does!)

Perhaps a couple of the things you try will eventually make it into a structure—but until then, how might you freestyle a life in connection to God?

And what happens if you don't?

My friend the Paralympian, who you met in chapter eight, can answer this for you. When he landed at the Paris Olympics in 2024 and was competing in multiple events, he felt the pressure of being on a global stage. He thought maybe he had to change up who he was. "I was trying to add on more spiritual disciplines than normal, trying to do and be and talk like what I thought was spiritually perfect, because I thought that's what I needed to do for such a big moment in my life. But I was too in my head, I was trying to be someone I wasn't, doing things I never do—and I know it affected me in the competition for the hundred meters. I had to be myself."

So he stopped trying to be someone else. He surrendered to God. He steered into the skid of who he was. He regained his focus. And in his events later that week, he won two silver medals.

He told me, "The truth is, there's some weekly structure I have in my time with God. And there's a lot that is sporadic and flowing during the week too. I have a bit of both. And I have to be myself."

We learn from my friend who lost her daughter and my friend who lost his leg and went on to compete in the Paralympics—the point isn't to have a perfect structure in anyone else's eyes. The point is to stay connected to the Source of life and to flourish. You may do it differently than others, and you might do it differently than yourself in different seasons. And that's not just okay, that is awesome. This freestyle might just set you free.

Revival at a Catholic Funeral

I had not attended a church service in months.

I was on the road nonstop, at conferences during the week. And I was preaching on Sundays, so I was *at* churches, but I had not attended a service. I had not been in a room with other people praising God. This was not the norm, and this was not ideal, and I could feel it weighing on me. At some of the events or services, I had responsibilities or needed to have important conversations before I spoke, so I could not enter the worship service. Other times I was praying with a lovely person I met in the lobby or answering insightful questions from staff members backstage. All to say, my time was filled with meaningful conversations. No time was wasted. But for those reasons, I had not actively taken part in a church service or been in the music part of worship for months.

I missed it. I needed it. I wanted an encounter with God alongside His people. Encountering God in large and lively rooms of people isn't even my natural bent. But now, without it, I was starved for it.

While on the road, Guy and I received word that my mother-in-law's relative had passed away. She was elderly and loved, and though we didn't personally know her, the service was only a few hours away from our route on the road. We decided to attend the funeral, which would take place at a Catholic church.

I had been weary for weeks because I had not worshiped

God in community in some time. As an introspective person who can constantly be in my head, worshiping God out loud brings the conversation from me and my thoughts, to me and God. I can't talk badly to myself when I'm talking to God. I can't think of the worst-case scenarios when I am thinking of God. I can't declare hopelessness when I am declaring hopefulness. Because of how I am wired, when I don't have space to worship God, I can feel less like myself, disconnected from Him, and too in my head about everything else.

That morning I prayed, *I want an encounter with You today, God. Whatever it looks like, I will take it. I am going to look for it.*

And that's what I did.

I prayed for it and looked for it . . . as my husband and I ate breakfast at a Best Western. As we drove a couple of hours through zero scenery. As we arrived at a church made of stone. As people dressed in black greeted one another in tender sadness. To be fair, it was not a totally bleak affair. Since we were mourning the loss of someone who had lived a long and beautiful life, no one seemed to be harboring regrets between family members or things left unsaid. People were respectful but also very happy to see each other; the friends and family were warm and welcoming, hugging everyone who walked in.

Still, we were all attending a funeral in a Catholic church.

I have been to several Catholic funerals. I know my experience is my own and I cannot speak for everyone, so this may not be *your* experience, but for *me*, this has never been a place where I've had a fresh encounter with the Holy Spirit.

And yet I was praying for it and looking for it. And I found it.

As every part of the liturgy was read, I internalized each word and repeated each one out loud with all my heart. With the songs sung, I sang from the depths of my gut, thinking about what the words meant and honestly relaying them to God as if we were having a face-to-face conversation. When asked to reflect, I truly did. With moments of silence and prayer, I was brought to tears. My husband looked at me and asked if I was okay. We quietly chuckled (I'm truly sorry if that was inappropriate; we are not crushing it). But I had not been able to encounter God like that for months. Kneeling in the pew, I lifted my hands as I prayed. Thanking God for the moment. Telling Him how I trusted Him. Surrendering my life to Him. He felt so close. It turns out, we were having a conversation after all.

After the service, more warm hugs and smiles ensued as introductions continued with Guy's distant relatives. We snacked on some of those bite-sized sandwiches you get from Costco. (The ones that are barely sandwiches . . . they're wrapped in a tortilla like a wheel, and I think they have cream cheese in them? If you know, you know.) And you know what? I also felt God's presence while surrounded by this warm community. I heard reminders of God's faithfulness as I learned about our late family member's life. I felt the joy of the Lord as I met and laughed along with once-distant relatives who now felt close. As Guy and I drove away, I told him what a powerful experience I'd had with God. And he laughed. "I know."

When you go on a scavenger hunt for an encounter with God, you will find one.

When you go on a scavenger hunt for an encounter with God, you will find one.

He is not hiding from us. He is not locked behind a secret door with a secret code. If we want God, we can have God. God will draw close where He is wanted.

Now, let's be real. I could have said, "I want God . . . but I want God in a church building I'm more accustomed to, with aesthetics that are more my vibe, with worship songs and lyrics

I already know and love, with traditions in the service that I prefer, with the most flavorful after-church snacks (fresh-made fingerfoods you can't buy in bulk), with a community that looks like me, talks like me, and has known me for a long time. *That* is what it will take for me to have an encounter with God. Until then, I will wait."

I am so glad I did not wait.

You can experience God right where you are.

In a church you've never been to, with people you don't yet know, and through songs that are unfamiliar. With music in a worship style or genre that is not your favorite. Through a sermon that is not perfectly tailored to the moment you're in but is more for someone else in the room. With people who may not relate to you or understand your background or lifestyle.

You can experience God in your home. You can tell your family you need alone time in your bedroom for ten minutes, then get on your knees at the side of your bed and ask God for help. You can pray in the shower. You can pray while you garden. You can pray as you accompany your kids to the park, library, or museum down the road.

If we want God, we can have God.

You can experience God at a Best Western, on the least scenic drive ever, and at a traditional Catholic funeral. I know it.

God says, "You will seek me and find me when you search for me with all your heart."[5]

Another translation puts it this way: "When you come looking for me, you'll find me. Yes, when you get serious about finding me and want it more than anything else, I'll make sure you won't be disappointed."[6]

A way to pray and play in goblet, especially in seasons without routines or predictability, is to tell God, "I want an encounter with You today—whatever that looks like." Pray for it. And look for it. God says, "When you want Me, you will have Me. When you are truly searching for Me, you will find Me." It will be a successful scavenger hunt.

Our expectations to have the most elite routines ever are exhausting, and they do not come from God. Our expectations on churches to be perfectly attuned to our tastes, wants, and desires will leave us hoping that the church is catering to us instead of to God. Our expectations of our lives, our faith, and our communities of faith might become unrealistic and ultimately disappointing. I will say the same about moments with God. Don't put the pressure on every encounter with God to be the most emotional, eye-opening, transformational moment of your life. Instead, expect the goodness of God. The peace of God. The joy of God. Expect that the pursuit of God is part of encountering the presence of God. Search for Him, then enjoy the small ways you encounter His presence in your everyday life.

This is the best scavenger hunt we could ever want to be a part of. *Pray, play, in goblet.* You *can* encounter and enjoy God at Best Westerns. At the Olympics. In unpretty prayers in the middle of the night. And alongside pinwheel sandwiches from Costco with a new favorite relative you just met.

PLAY

1. What are some ways to encounter God that you've already experienced and loved?
2. What are things you want to try out this month to enjoy God in a new way?

Write out details of how you will "pray and play" in Your Personal Shortcut on page 219.

CHAPTER 16

Prune

"HOW DO I REFRESH?"

After years of teaching on the importance of spend-ing real time with Jesus in our own way and building our own trellis, I thought that was the end of my revelation of "abiding." I could hear the exhale in the rooms I taught in as I told people that they might be carrying weights they weren't carrying ten years ago, and they may need a new structure, new supports, and a new trellis. I felt the grace leave my mouth, and I watched as it landed on my brothers' and sisters' ears as we realized together that we were being invited into a fresh kind of relationship with God.

So you'd think I would have been prepared when a woman at an event in Florida raised her hand and asked, "How do I start a new trellis?"

She continued, "I want to do this! So how would I do it? How would a vinedresser undo branches, untwine the growth, dismantle a trellis, and start a new one to help support all the new fruit? How do I flourish *now*?"

It was an amazing question. I was not prepared. After that event, I set out to discover the answer. I'll tell you now: It's not what I expected.

Months later I was with my supercool lab coat queen in Paso Robles, attempting to dig up some more answers. She affirmed that different vineyards with different manifestations of growth needed different structures to hold them up. In other words, she confirmed my recent discovery that sometimes we are bearing so much fruit that we need a new trellis. Sometimes we are growing so much that we need a new structure. And sometimes our old structures don't work for us anymore.

So I asked her how to start a new trellis when there's already so much growth.

"That's the wrong question," she said. "It sounds to me like you need to prune."

The Truth About Flourishing

Up until that point, I'd understood pruning in a very elementary way. As I mentioned, I have a fig tree in my backyard, and when it gets overgrown, the leaves appear less healthy and we have to trim them back. In other words, we prune them. This way, the leaves come back healthier and fuller, and we get better figs as a result. This isn't the *most* scientific way to explain this, of course. Again, rookie gardener here.

But one thing that's been clear to me for some time is this: Trimming is needed for transformation. Pruning is needed for flourishing to be possible.

When it came to grapes on a vine, I wasn't as well informed. I wondered if Jesus' analogy would break down here. After all, it's a metaphor, and perhaps it goes only so far. I know Jesus wants us to bear fruit, so the idea that we would prune branches bearing fruit just didn't make sense to me. And since my awesome winemaker/scientist friend didn't know the context of the scripture I was decoding, I wondered if her expertise with vines wouldn't be enough to solve my fruit-pruning puzzle. Maybe pruning wasn't as important for those of us who wanted to "abide" in the vine, right?

Wrong.

I asked her, "Is the point of pruning to grow more grapes? As many grapes as possible?"

She looked at me in her marshmallow-white lab coat and smiled. It was clear that I had half-knowledge about what I was talking about and still had lots to learn. She was patient with me, though, and so very gracious. "No, the goal is not to grow as many grapes as possible," she said.

Well, I thought, *there goes the entire analogy.*

She continued, "The goal is never to produce the *most* fruit. The goal is to produce *good* fruit."

The goal is never to produce the *most* fruit. The goal is to produce *good* fruit.

Good Fruit

At the beginning of John 15, Jesus says, "I am the true vine, and my Father is the gardener. He cuts off every branch in me that bears no fruit, while every branch that does bear fruit he prunes so that it will be even more fruitful."[1]

It turns out that even before Jesus talked about abiding in the vine and remaining in Him, He first talked about Himself as the Vine (the Source of life) and God as the Gardener. He talked about fruit-bearing branches and their need to be pruned.

He said that God is the One who examines the branches and trims away what is bearing no fruit. But He is also examining the parts of our lives that bear a lot of fruit, to see what must be pruned so we can be even more fruitful.

In his commentary on the Gospels, J. Carl Laney says that Jesus is teaching "that as the vinedresser cuts away and removes that which would hinder the productivity of the vine, so God the Father, through loving discipline, removes things from the lives of believers that hinder their spiritual fruitfulness."[2]

While the Greek word *kathairō* is translated "to prune," it could just as well be translated "to cleanse."[3]

God wants to cleanse anything hindering your growth. He also wants to rid you of the seemingly small things that are slowly poisoning your growth, the beginnings of what could infest and infect your whole life.

Robin Murto, a grape grower in Yamhill County, Oregon, said, "Pruning is the single most important job you can do in a vineyard. What eventually ends up in a bottle of wine starts right here." Dick Shea, another grape grower in Oregon, notes, "Pruning isn't something that seems to intrigue people, but it is just absolutely critical. It's integral to the quality of the grapes."[4]

A lot of smart people who know a lot more about growing grapes than I do insist that pruning is an essential part of good fruit production.

My cool wine scientist friend in Paso Robles said, "If you're not in the business of growing vineyards, you might assume the goal is to have more quantity, but that would be incorrect. The goal is to have quality. The goal is not to have an impressive-looking vineyard for tourists to drive by or take pictures at. The goal is to make great wine."

Simply put: We cannot have a flourishing life while still holding tight to what holds us back.

If we do not allow God to examine our hearts, examine our fruit, and prune away the poison, trim away the unhealth, and cut back the overgrowth, we will be in danger of being very productive . . . in all the wrong things. We could be producing unhealthiness in our churches, bitterness in our hearts, or exhausting environments in our homes. We could have lives that look like they are flourishing but are decaying from the inside. We could produce fruit that looks aesthetically appealing to people but offers them no substance. If you and I do not learn the importance of pruning in our lives, we can bear much fruit of the *unhealthy* variety.

We cannot have a flourishing life while still holding tight to what holds us back.

God is looking for good fruit.

Jesus said, "You did not choose me, but I chose you and appointed you so that you might go and bear fruit—fruit that will last."[5]

Another translation says,

> You have not chosen Me, but I have chosen you and I have appointed *and* placed *and* purposefully planted you, so that you would go and bear fruit *and* keep on bearing, and that your fruit will remain *and* be lasting, so that whatever you ask of the Father in My name [as My representative] He may give to you.[6]

Jesus said, "I am after good fruit. I am not after all the fruit possible. I am not here to see the most productivity possible. Having the most fruit is not the goal. Good fruit is."

Then He says something unexpected: that your fruit should also remain in Him. Your fruit should also carry the character of

Jesus. Your fruit should be surrendered to the will of God. Your fruit should not serve any purpose outside of glorifying God. Your fruit should remain connected to Jesus, with God's Spirit giving it life.

Some of us have connected to Jesus, abided in Jesus, flourished in Jesus, but have started to serve the fruit. We have started to aim for a fruitful life instead of one connected to the Source. Or we were once connected to the Source, and then saw fruit, and decided to try to sustain our lives from the fruit instead of the Vine. But no matter how beautiful, tasty, and luxurious that fruit looks, and no matter how appealing, impressive, and even helpful the fruit of your life is, your life cannot be sustained by the fruit. You will have a full and flourishing life only when you are sustained by the source of the fruit—the Vine. The fruit is the outcome of a life connected to Jesus. The fruit is not the Vine.

So what is the answer to my new friend's question?

How do we flourish *now*? Do we need new trellises? Perhaps. Do we need new rhythms? Maybe. But here is the first thing we need to do: Prune. Trim. Cut away.

The answer is not to add more weight. The answer is to first let go of what no longer contributes to the flourishing of your life. The answer is to surrender. King David gave us a prayer we can pray:

> Search me, God, and know my heart;
> test me and know my anxious thoughts.
> See if there is any offensive way in me,
> and lead me in the way everlasting.[7]

I love how another translation says, "Explore me, O God, and know the real me."[8]

If we want a real relationship with God, we have to stop thinking that it's about producing as much as possible, or to stop thinking it's about looking as good as possible. No. No. No. Turn away from that way of thinking. It's not about the aesthetics, it's not about the volume. It's about the health of what your life is producing.

The answer might not be a new structure. The answer might be to allow God to examine your life's fruit and cut off anything that is no longer connected to Him. You may be the most productive person in the world, producing lots of . . . *sour fruit.*

This process isn't about adding on. It's about taking off.

Here are the questions we must all ask ourselves:

What do I need to let go of?

What unhealthy growth do I need to prune?

The truth is, it might be an unhealthy relationship.

It might be an unhealthy relationship with a drink, a drug, or a device.

It might be the need to impress. It might be the longing for applause.

It might be unhealthy habits.

It might be trying to be the person you were ten years ago. Or constantly putting your life on hold until it's exactly where you want it to be ten years from now.

What do you need to let go of?

You can build the most impressive trellis in the world. You can plan out all the strongest supports seamlessly. But Jesus mentioned pruning first. Why? He was not saying we will not flourish without it. He was saying we will be in danger of flourishing at the wrong things.

Today, what do you need to cut off, turn from, and lay down at the feet of Jesus?

Surrender is a shortcut to God.

Pruning Equals Growing

There came a day when my husband and I felt called to *more*. I thought, *That's a no for me, dawg. There's no way that's true.* I don't mean *more* in a public way—just called to more things with our families, our church, and yes, some things in our jobs and our ministries. But none of it seemed right because of *other* things God had said. He had also called us to rest. He'd called us to have a healthy marriage. He'd called us to have lives of joy. This is all in God's Word.

Knowing all these other things God had called us to, no one who knew us well would have agreed that God was probably calling us to *more*.

We were at capacity. We had no more margin. There was only one thing I could think to do. I told my husband, "God will have to increase our capacity."

Does God do that? How does that work?

For weeks we asked God to grow our capacity.

And day after day, what came to mind as I prayed were things I could let go of. Things I was doing that I was not called to do. Things I was called to do ten years ago that I was *no longer* called to do. People I loved and was making lots of time for but was no longer called to make as much exceptional time for. Does this sound harsh? It was.

Pruning isn't always pretty.

I could not please everyone *and* please God. Someone was getting the least of me, and it was the One who'd created me and called me.

I had to let go of some things that were good things. Great things. Things other people would never tell me to let go of. But those good things were standing in the way of God things—things God was actually calling me to do. The truth? Other people were called to do some of the things I was taking on. I was bearing fruit that was not mine, and it was weighing me down.

After a time of saying no (ouch) and letting go of some things I had taken on as my sole responsibility, we found more time and, yes, more capacity. We were able to say yes to things I'd never imagined possible. We had made more space in our lives and more space for the Holy Spirit, and by His power and might we were able to take on another level of growth.

Today, I encourage you:

Let go of the things you were never called to.

Let go of the things you were once called to but no longer are.

Some of your fruit is not *good fruit* and is weighing you down.

Ask God to examine it and bring to mind what is not from Him.

Ask God to examine the ways your motivation has become your fruit instead of the Vine.

Then surrender it. Give it to God. Invite Him to rearrange the interiors of your life. To direct you toward the right *no*. To direct you toward the right *yes*.

Good fruit will begin to grow in and through your life as you surrender to God.

I am thankful for the scientist I met in Paso Robles. She opened my eyes to think differently about real growth. Somber and aware of how much I still have to learn about vines, I looked at her and said, "Thank you. I've got it now. The best thing for vines is a life of constant pruning."

"No, that's not what I said," she replied. "They *do* need to be pruned, but there's a season for that. Their whole life is not just about pruning. To be clear, there's a harvest coming."

PRUNE

1. What expectations have you placed on yourself that do not come from God?
2. What things are standing in the way of closeness with God, closeness with others, or flourishing in your life?
3. What things are weighing on you? With all you learned about pruning, what do you need to surrender to God today? Right here and right now, give it to Him.

Write out what you want to "prune" and surrender to God today in Your Personal Shortcut on page 219.

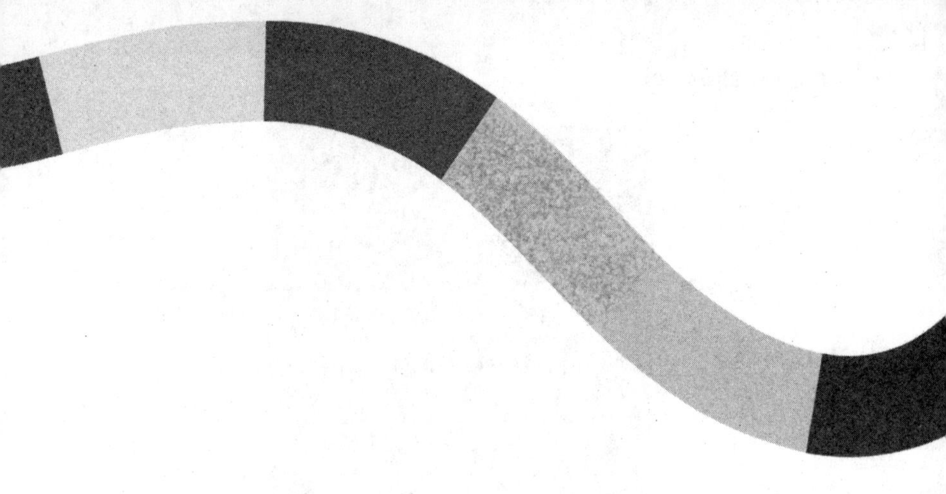

Your Personal Shortcut

It's time to build Your Personal Shortcut! Turn the page to discover your best way to experience God in your specific season. If you haven't filled out your answers yet, do it now! I've included an example for you as well. Start with surrender and pruning. Play, pray, and try some ways to encounter God. Plan for rhythms of untangling, engaging, and closeness in your specific schedule, in your personal trellis. Always keep your praise-o-nality and personality in mind. Your shortcut might change in different seasons. And that is a good thing.

PERSONALITY

nostalgic

love time alone

love hiking, beach, outdoors

I love planning dinner parties and outings with friends

PRAISE-O-NALITY

interior expert
recreationalist
artist of people

PERSONAL STRUCTURE

In a busy season. Planning for this week, and after that I want to plan for a month! I want to include my praise-o-nalities now!

PRACTICAL SUPPORTS

This week, reading Bible and prayer 4 days, worship, rest, and celebration 1 day. Building out the trellis calendar to include all rhythms next month!

S	M	T	W	T	F	S
church + rest, afternoon hike	morning prayer + God's Word		evening walks listening to God's Word + praying			dinner at ho celebr Elijal promo

PLAY

Going on a scavenger hunt for God. Saying yes to visiting friend's small group. Inviting friends to go on walks with me.

PRUNE

I am surrendering my expectations of what I thought my life should look like/timeline I thought I should have. I'm ready to embrace the life I have and enjoy God in it.

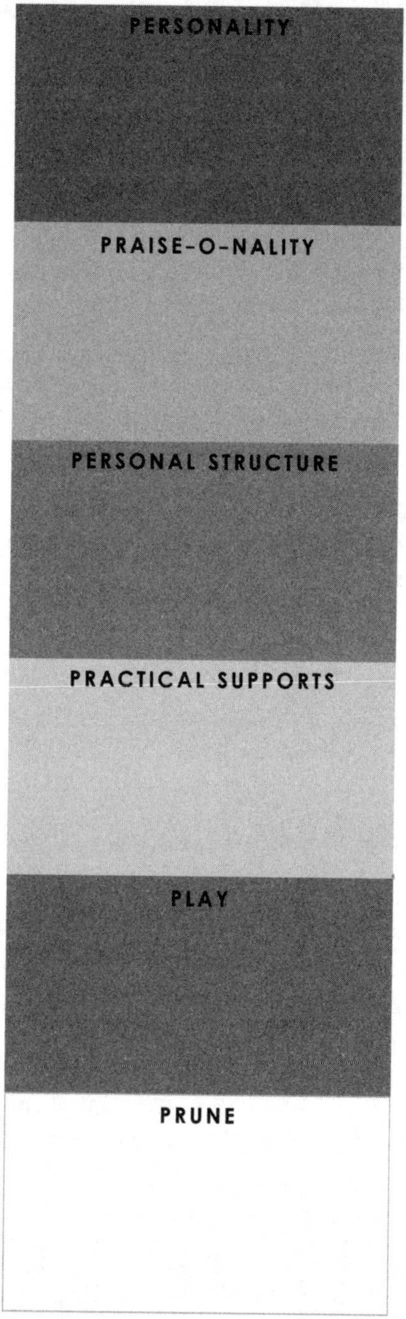

PERSONALITY

PRAISE-O-NALITY

PERSONAL STRUCTURE

PRACTICAL SUPPORTS

PLAY

PRUNE

Part 4

The Great Uncomplicating

CHAPTER 17

How Do I Know If This Is Real for Me?

Since I couldn't quit asking sweet Niccolò questions about vineyards and trellises down to our very last minutes together, it seems only fitting that these days I now get my own fair share of questions about abiding in the Vine. I only wish I'd been more prepared for this one:

"How do I know if I'm really connected to God?"

I wasn't ready for it. Wide-eyed and filled with hope and curiosity, a kind woman in Minnesota continued with a follow-up: "I know I love Jesus, yet something in me feels off. Is there any way to know when I'm really connected?"

The curious questioner and her friends were gathered around me, and she was telling me she'd read the same Bible and prayed every day at the same time in the morning for three decades. Yet she felt her relationship with God had grown stale and routine—so the idea of breaking through roadblocks, unlocking her shortcuts, pruning what she was not meant to carry, and starting a new structure felt like new life in her veins. But now she wanted to know *how to measure* if that new structure was working.

Certainly, we don't want to view our connection with God as a destination—a place where we arrive—rather than an ongoing and authentic relationship with Him. But semantics aside, I understood the question she was asking. She was not new to God. She was experienced with God. *But she was not enjoying God.* And she wanted to know: How do I know if, after implementing these personal pivots, I am *truly* connected to God?

Does such a measure exist?

Yes, it does.

I had to dig beyond my current understanding of "abide" to get there. But once I found it, I couldn't believe I had ever taught abiding with Jesus without it.

It is in John 15 where we learned that as *branches* we must be connected to the Source of life—the Vine—to live, thrive, and flourish. That part we've covered. But what was new information to me was the word used here for branches: κλῆμα or *kléma*. Upon further study, I learned that this is the only place in the Bible where this specific word is used. Jesus is referring to a very specific kind of branch. This word emphasizes two things about this particular branch: *tenderness* and *flexibility*.[1]

Are you *tender*?

Are you *flexible*?

Oh, how I wish the questions were different. I'd much prefer to be asked, "Are you making deadlines?" or "Are you producing beyond people's expectations?" If those were the measures, then at least there would be ways I could work harder, wake up earlier, or just rest less than other people to get more done. But this? The way to know I'm a branch truly connected to Jesus is if I'm tender or flexible?

Oh, no.

As I read these two words, I had to stop and consider my temperament even this past week. The ways I'd been irritable, short, judgmental, selfish, prideful, and holding on tightly to my expectations of people and my personal preferences that I deemed perfect. I could see that while I love Jesus, and I'm in a real relationship with Him, I am not always demonstrating the characteristics of a person living at home in His presence.

That kind woman in Minnesota was on to something.

Tender and Flexible

How about you? Have you ever wondered how your relationship with God is *really* going?

As it turns out, the Word of God gives us a few good ways to measure our spiritual maturity and our true intimacy with God. It tells us there are literal actions that come out of our lives when God's Spirit lives in us and we are connected to Jesus. I was shocked as I read some passages I had known for a long time, now with a new lens. I was amazed at how well these words paired with tenderness and flexibility.

> What happens when we live God's way? He brings gifts into our lives, much the same way that fruit appears in an orchard—things like affection for others, exuberance about life, serenity. We develop a willingness to stick with things, a sense of compassion in the heart, and a conviction that a basic holiness permeates things and people. We find ourselves involved in loyal commitments, not needing to force our way in life, able to marshal and direct our energies wisely.[2]

Another translation puts it like this: "The Holy Spirit produces a different kind of fruit: *unconditional* love, joy, peace, patience, kindheartedness, goodness, faithfulness, gentleness, and self-control."[3]

These are the good fruits—the actions that come out of a life that is connected to God, through Jesus, and filled with the Holy Spirit.

So how *can* we know if we are truly connected to God, allowing His Spirit to move in and through us?

Here are some questions to help you measure:

- When there's a change of plans, do you quickly derail? Or are you able to be flexible and let go of your expectations?
- When someone going through a hard time opens up to you, do you rush to get out of the conversation as quickly as possible? Or are you tender, willing to be uncomfortable, and possibly a bit late for the next thing you need to do? How present and compassionate are you willing to be for someone who longs to feel seen?
- When someone doesn't agree with you, are you quick to judge, cut them off, and make them feel less-than? Or are you able to be kind and treat them as if they are loved by God and their feelings are important to Him? If they are cutting you off and rude to you, are you able to graciously excuse yourself and, once you walk away, shoot a prayer up for them and move on?
- When someone hurts you, are you quick to hurt them back? Are you mentally rehearsing a list of things you would like to say to them—perfect comebacks to make them feel small? Or do you demonstrate self-control, considering what words or actions would or would not be helpful in this situation? Are you able to see what would cause more division and what might cause more unity or peace—and choose the latter?

- When you're in a difficult season at home or at work, do you lash out at others, treat everyone like they're against you, and live on the defense? Or do you try to find ways to bring joy to people and peace to situations? Further, do you allow others to do the same for you?
- Do you have an exuberance about life, a peace and a joy that surpass all understanding, overflowing in a way that makes others want what you have?

These are very broad examples, and they may not all apply to you. I don't know every specific situation in your life. But I know that the Word of God gives us a framework of what kind of posture we will have toward others when we are truly and intimately connected to Him. It's not a perfected schedule and it's not pristine rhythms. It's a tender, selfless, and open-handed life of actively loving God and others well. It's active, good fruit.

(Not) Real Faith

We learned earlier in this book that the Pharisees and religious people of Jesus' day *looked* like they were connected to God—yet they were some of the least gracious, most unkind people. So clearly, looking holy doesn't make you holy.

Looking holy doesn't make you holy.

In Matthew 23, Jesus outlined some specific ways the religious people tried to flaunt their faith and seem the most connected to God, but their actions proved they were not. He revealed how . . .

1. They know how to teach it but not how to live it.

Jesus called their faith a "veneer," exposing how they had polished speech but didn't "live it out in their behavior."[4]

Jesus was saying we can teach the Word of God beautifully without actually doing what God's words tell us to do. We can post online about the great things we're doing, or shout about all our good deeds in public, while never truly serving others or spending real time with God in private. We must radically resist the temptation to live a double life.

2. They put burdens on people instead of lifting burdens off people.

Jesus pointed out how they "seem to take pleasure" in weighing others down and giving people more rules, yet "wouldn't think of lifting a finger to help."[5]

They loved piling religious to-do lists onto people . . . without telling them *how* to accomplish those things. Without walking alongside them. Without empowering them practically and holistically to live a free life. Instead, they make it harder, add rules and regulations that don't come from God, and *enjoy* it.

Jesus did not come to give us burdens. He came to take our burdens away. When we claim to follow Jesus but create environments that make people feel heavier with shame instead of lighter in freedom, we are doing it wrong.

3. They care more about how people see them than letting others know they are seen.

Jesus also said, "Their lives are perpetual fashion shows, embroidered prayer shawls one day and flowery prayers the next. They love to sit at the head table at church dinners, basking in the most prominent positions, preening in the radiance of public flattery."[6]

In the name of worshiping God, the religious elite of Jesus' day created a culture of worshiping themselves. They were obsessed with their own press and what people thought of their name more than they cared about lifting up God's name.

Jesus was not saying that things done in public are wrong, not at all. God moves in and through people publicly all the time. Jesus was speaking against doing something *only* to be seen. This means doing something you wouldn't have done had it been in a more private setting.

Only you know in your heart if you are doing something just to be seen. Make sure you are serving people to serve people. Worshiping God to worship God. In private *and* in public.

4. They spend more time pretending to be compassionate than being compassionate.

Jesus was bringing light to the fact that some people would rather go out of their way to *seem* helpful than to spend their time actually helping people. Jesus exposed the religious people, saying, "What you say is not what you do. You steal the homes from under the widows while you pretend to pray for them."[7]

He was calling out religious people who publicly prayed for suffering people but did nothing to alleviate that suffering. Worse, some might actually have been taking advantage of broken systems while publicly speaking against those systems that served them. Jesus was saying, "You like to be praised for how you talk about justice. You don't care about justice actually being carried out."

5. They care more about people following them than following God.

Jesus said, "You go halfway around the world to make a convert, but once you get him you make him into a replica of yourselves."[8]

The religious elite were known for caring more about their cause than caring for the kingdom of God. They cared more about people becoming followers of the Pharisees than becoming

The goal is not to make people students of *you*. The goal is to make students of *Jesus*.

followers of Christ. Jesus was clarifying that the goal is not to make people students of *you*. The goal is to make students of *Jesus*. Disciples of Jesus. Followers of Jesus. If you are constantly selling *your* way of living to people instead of pointing them toward *Jesus'* way of living, you are selling people short.

6. They care more about executing spiritual acts than living a spirit-filled life.

Jesus went there. He said, "You keep meticulous account books, tithing on every nickel and dime you get, but on the meat of God's Law, things like fairness and compassion and commitment—the absolute basics!—you carelessly take it or leave it. Careful book-keeping is commendable, but the basics are required."[9]

Jesus is *not* against sacred rhythms of obedience—quite the opposite! He lived a life celebrating the Sabbath, in prayer, and engaging in God's Word. In regard to the practice of generosity, it might be one of Jesus' favorites. He shared about wisdom with money and not making money our god. And the religious elite took this practice seriously as well. They knew tithing was important, but they forgot that the practices were not the point. They were a means to an end. So despite their rigorous practices, they lacked love and compassion. Some might say they were *crushing it*, but *incomplete*.

7. They care about the outside more than the inside.

Jesus called out the duplicity of the religious people of His day, saying, "You remove fine layers of film and dust from the outside of a cup or bowl, but you leave the inside full of *greed and* covetousness and self-indulgence."[10]

Jesus was saying some people care more about their outward appearance than the interior of their heart.

God, don't let it be us.

We must resist the temptation to obsess over the exterior of our lives while overlooking the state of our interior lives. We want to love God and enjoy God in the hidden places of our lives first. True transformation will then overflow to the outside of our lives. And rest assured: *That* is the proper order.

Love Is the Measure

I have no idea if your relationship with God is real and thriving or burned-out and dry. You don't know if mine is either. You don't know if your kid's is. Is your wife's relationship real? Is your husband's thriving? Is your pastor's? I don't know. Neither do you. I want to emphasize this: This list is not for the purposes of measuring someone else's relationship with God. This, my friend, is for you.

The question is not, How can I tell if this is real for *them*?

That leads to an exhausting life driven by judgmental behaviors, religious pride, and moral superiority. That's the last thing we want for our lives.

The question from the beginning of this book has been, How can I tell if this is real for *me*?

Jesus Himself gave us this measure: "Your love for one another will prove to the world that you are my disciples."[11]

The Pharisees got it wrong.

Jesus did not say that *impressing* people would be the measure.

Jesus said *loving* people is the measure.

Reading your Bible more than other people does not make you a better follower of Jesus.

Volunteering at church more than other people in your family does not make you a better follower of Jesus.

Your life's trellis can be truly impressive. Your routines can be perfectly planned, and you can live them out flawlessly.

You can be the King of Spiritual Disciplines.

The Queen of Structure and Rhythms.

But if these rhythms do not help you be with Jesus Himself, and if they don't make you more like Jesus, and they're not resulting in a life of more active, tangible, patient, grace-filled, forgiving, and tender love for people, then none of your practices matter. Your accomplishments hold no weight in light of eternity.

Love is the measure.

Love is the measure.

In 1 Corinthians 13, we learn that we are not the first generation who might have thought that seeming the most spiritual or being the most skilled would be the goal. Paul clarifies:

> What if I speak in the *most elegant* languages of people or in the *exotic* languages of the heavenly messengers, but I live without love? Well then, anything I say is like the clanging of brass or a crashing cymbal. What if I have the gift of prophecy, am blessed with knowledge and insight to all the mysteries, or what if my faith is strong enough to scoop a mountain *from its bedrock*, yet I live without love? If so, I am nothing. I could give all that I have to feed the poor, I could surrender my body to be burned *as a martyr*, but if I do not live in love, I gain nothing *by my selfless acts*.[12]

What if your spiritual routines are perfect? What if you raise your hands the highest? What if you post the most scriptures out of everyone you know on Facebook?

None of those are signs of a life connected to God.

Paul went on to describe what love truly is and what a life of real love actually looks like. If I were to replace the word *love* with *you* in this passage of Scripture, this is what *your* life would look like when you're actively loving others:

> You are patient; you are kind. You aren't envious, don't boast, *brag, or strut about.* There's no arrogance in you; you're never rude, crude, or indecent—you're not self-absorbed. You're not easily upset. You don't tally wrongs or celebrate injustice; but truth—*yes, truth*—is your delight! You put up with anything and everything that comes along; you trust, hope, and endure no matter what.[13]

This would be proof of a life connected to God.

Love is not theoretical. It's active. And practical.

Just in case the kind woman in Minnesota picks up this book, I want her to know she challenged me to dig deeper into what Jesus says is the most important measure of a relationship with Him. To her I say—*thank you.*

If you were to ask me today, "How do we know if we are connected to God for real?" I would say, "Are you tender and flexible?"

Are you tender and flexible with *others*? Are you tender toward those who are hurting, insecure, or need grace? Are you flexible when things don't go the way you planned? Are you quick to forgive? Slow to burst out in anger and slow to hold on to offense?

Are you tender and flexible with *yourself*? Are you receiving the grace God has for you? Or are you spiraling in the shame that Jesus already came to set you free from? Have you given your burdens to Jesus? Are you resting in the knowledge that you are already loved before you do one thing?

Are you tender and flexible with *God*? Are you spending real time with Him, and are you tender toward the Holy Spirit's leading? Are you flexible when God uses someone you wouldn't choose or when His plans are on a different timeline from yours? Are you flexible and obedient to what God calls you to do?

The truth is that "to love God means that we keep His commands, and His commands don't weigh us down."[14] To love God means to obey God, and the good news is that what He asks of us isn't heavy enough to break us apart. Spend real time with God, obey God, and love people. Be tender and flexible with others, yourself, and with your holy Father.

Love is the measure.

How can I measure if it's real for you? I can't. But you can look at the interior of your own life; honestly reflect on your time, your obedience to God, and your posture toward people; come to God humble and surrendered; and get to the point in your life where you can say,

"This is real for me."

CHAPTER 18

How Do I Make Sure This Lasts?

A few years ago, Guy and I took up boxing classes. Our class is led by two trainers we both love and hate, depending on the workout routine. (I kid. A little.) I have old-school, dark brown boxing gloves that remind me of something out of *Rocky*, and somehow hard things feel easier when you low-key love your outfit. Our trainers lead us through three rounds of power punching and rhythm punching with our individual punching bags; and three intervals of mobility, flexibility, and strength training with weights. We go back and forth for about an hour. It's the best and the absolute worst.

Throughout my first year of these classes, one thing in our training baffled me. During our punching rounds, we always did a few minutes of power punching (a different routine every day where we are hitting with as much power as we can) and then a few minutes of rhythm punching (a different routine every day where we are hitting lightly, but on a rhythm, which also requires moving our feet and waists to the music playing).

I asked one of our trainers, "Why do we always do these back-to-back? Power *and* rhythm?"

"Because that's boxing, dawg," he quipped.

I laughed and clarified my question. "Explain it to me like I'm a ten-year-old. What is the danger if I do only one?"

"In boxing," he explained, "you need to know how to throw power punches to knock your opponent out. You need the technique and the strength to do so. These rounds help you with power."

"So don't I just need power?"

"Well, let's say I'm your opponent, and I know you are just good at power. So when you come at me with power punches, I'll just move," he said. "If you have only strength but not flexibility, then your opponent will try to outmaneuver you. He will hope you run out of breath chasing him around. That's why you have the rhythm round. If you have all the power in the world but don't have a good pace, you'll lose due to exhaustion."

Whoa.

He continued, "And if you have only rhythm—you move a lot, have a ton of energy, and can fight for a long time—but have no power, you won't make an impact. You can stay in the ring longer than other people while still doing nothing. You need power *and* rhythm. You need them all to make an impact and keep going."

This is the same with our faith.

Pace with No Power

After we start to have a thriving relationship with God—flourishing and seeing our good fruit—our next natural questions might be, *How do I make sure this lasts? How does this stay real?*

For those of us who have put little to no intention into our walks with God, I would suggest a set of rhythms to help you start. In other words, it's trellis time. But our lives cannot be sustained through rhythms alone. Our faith cannot be sustained through spiritual practices alone. We don't want to be in the ring longer than others while having no impact.

Perhaps we are flexible; when things don't go our way, we can brush it off and pivot. When someone doesn't do what they said they would do, we can forgive and not keep holding it against them. When there's chaos around us, we can still have peace within us and do our best to create peaceful environments as well.

But perhaps we have not scratched the surface of encountering the power of God in our lives. Perhaps we don't take inventory of the roadblocks in our lives and the apathy in our hearts and actively surrender them to God. We don't take risks in faith. We don't pray bold prayers. We've grown apathetic to the spiritual realm. We can move quickly and lightly, but we are not making the impact in our world and our communities that we've been called to make. We spend a long time in the ring, but without power.

I was recently with a friend and hero of mine, on a panel in a room of women in Los Angeles. We were about to answer questions on how to experience God in a fresh way. (*A great topic*, some might say. *Someone who is so cool she wore Princess Leia hairstyles in high school should probably write a book on that.*) Our panel was discussing if we should spend most of the time on spiritual practices, rhythms, and routines. I was all for it! *Let's just talk about that!*

And then my friend said this: "Look, we love spiritual practices. We all live them out, we all preach them, and we could all write ten books on them. And they are essential; no one is questioning that. But I don't want to spend all of our time on them. I'm weary of how Christ-followers are putting such an emphasis on their spiritual practices, and they are practicing them to death, but they do not have power. The power of God is not living *in* their life. The power and authority that comes from God is not being lived out *through* their life. We need to teach both. Let's split it up. Practices, yes, and also living with power and authority that comes from God, obeying Him when it's hard, and living a life of saying yes in faith."

Okay, I change my mind, I thought. *I take it back. I couldn't agree more.*

We need both.

Power but No Pace

Some of us have faith that is strong but not flexible.

When hard times come, we are resilient. When life is hard, we are tough. When we need a miracle, we are quick to ask God for it, believe God for it, and stand in faith that His kingdom will come and His will *will* be done on earth as it is in heaven. We pray boldly. We tell others to do so as well. We are strong, sturdy, and ready for battle.

But we are not flexible. When someone else isn't as strong as we are, we don't give them as much grace. When things don't turn out the way we hoped, or when our expectations aren't met, we get irritated, temperamental, and ungracious toward those around us. When someone lets us down, we are quick to let them know how displeased we are. We are slow to see someone else's side, and we are slow to forgive.

We claim to love God, but we don't, in fact, actively show love or patience or kindness to others.

We are quick to tell our loved ones, "Since we're in a fight right now, we need to stop and pray for the Holy Spirit to come down and help us! Let's bow our heads."

But we are slow to say, "I am sorry."

For some of us, it's easier to say we are relying on divine power than to sincerely consider our own posture.

Have you ever felt this way? I hate to admit it, but I certainly have. I have had strong faith while being inflexible with the people around me.

This is why we need both.

This is why, even in all of our different personalities and schedules and seasons and temperaments, it will be good for you to have some rhythms, seasonal commitments to stay in the presence of God, weeks where there's a plan, and a trellis to keep you in a humble posture and constant connection with Jesus.

And along with these supporting rhythms, we need power.

I'll say it: You need to do some things *out of rhythm*, in faith. You need to surrender to God the things that hold you back from Him. Say yes in risky obedience to things that take you out of your normal routine. Take steps toward forgiving the people who have hurt you. Pray for God to do something you have not seen done before. Start tithing at your church and trust God with your finances in a new way. Say yes to serving. Say yes to joining a small group. Say yes to texting that one person. Say yes to that hard thing God has been putting on your heart to do.

Pray for God to do something you have not seen done before.

This is for you to have an impact *and* to keep going.

Paul said,

> Test yourselves to make sure you are solid in the faith. Don't drift along taking everything for granted. Give yourselves

> regular checkups. You need firsthand evidence, not mere hearsay, that Jesus Christ is in you. Test it out. If you fail the test, do something about it.[1]

He continued: "*What's important is* not whether we appear to have passed the test, but that you do what is right *and act honorably* . . . Our prayer is *simple*: that you may be *whole and* complete."[2] There's that phrase again: *whole and complete.* Some might say *perfect.* With no fragments within your faith.

Paul was telling us to take honest inventory of our postures toward our lives, toward God, and toward others.

Are you living in the power and authority God has given you?

Are you tender *and* flexible?

Are you staying in the ring *while also* making an impact?

I love how another translation says this:

"Examine *and* test *and* evaluate your own selves to see whether you are holding to your faith *and* showing the proper fruits of it."[3]

(Are you tender *and* flexible?)

Look at your fruit. Look at the actions you are producing.

We don't want the enemy to have any victory in our lives by keeping us so content with our rhythms that we forget about our need for power.

And we don't want the enemy to have any victory in our lives by getting us out of the ring because we were bold and brave but simply ran out of breath.

Keep Going with Impact

As we finished up our final boxing interval with our trainer, we moved on to our final weight lifting reps of the day. I pulled off my worn-in, milk chocolate boxing gloves, wiped the sweat off my brow, and grabbed a weight.

"Go heavier," he insisted.

"How do you know I need to go heavier?"

He said, "Because I know what you can handle. I see how strong you are. But you keep staying at that one weight. You'll never get stronger that way."

I grabbed one weight above. He shook his head. I went one higher. He nodded.

"Explain to me why this is so important," I asked.

Aren't the people in my life so blessed to be answering my questions all the time?

"Like I said, you will never get stronger if you keep using the same weight. Of course you don't want to go too fast and you don't want to just lift what other people are lifting, but you have to know what you are capable of and when to engage your muscles appropriately. This helps with strength, this helps with posture, this helps with endurance. You started at a good place that was right for you, but you've stayed at this one weight all year. You can stay there, but nothing will change."

He was right. I could have lifted more earlier. But I didn't.

As I lifted my new weights, my muscles felt different. A higher weight was challenging, but it was within my ability. It was also good for me to learn that I would start feeling stagnant again, and perhaps bored too, if I didn't engage in new ways I was capable of.

After our weight training was over, our sweat was in puddles, and it was time to stretch. He walked over to me as if he assumed I would ask him why this was important too. *How did he know?*

He said, "We always end in a stretch so that you don't have muscle imbalances. We want to lengthen you back out. We worked on specific areas, and we don't want too much tension to build there. That will make you stiff. Stretching releases the tensions, improves circulation and blood flow, and helps your muscles recover. It also gives you a better range of motion. Over time, with weights *and* stretching, you will discover you can do more and move better and activate your muscles in new ways."

"So this is for longevity?" I asked. "Strength and health for the long haul?"

He said, "Oh, 1,000 percent. Otherwise you could get intensely strong . . . and then have a really intense injury. Some of the strongest people don't last long in the ring because they didn't make time to stretch."

I nodded. And pulled out my mat. And hurried to stretch. To the glory of God.

And in our lives, we need to do this too.

If you start to feel like your relationship with God is routine, mundane, and fruitless, or if you feel you're constantly producing fruit but you're always exhausted, here are some things to consider: power and rhythm. Also: weights and stretching.

Perhaps you need to add some weight.

I don't mean burdens you weren't meant to carry, or weights of guilt or shame, or expectations that come from other people but don't come from God. I mean God might be calling you to say yes to something new. He might be calling you to go deeper in your faith, to stretch yourself in trying a new rhythm, to add on a new support, to engage in a way you haven't before, to take on a new challenge, to share your faith with someone who has been on your heart, to pray again for something you've stopped praying for, or to say yes to something you have never seen done. This will help you grow as you have been created to grow. It's possible your faith has grown stale and routine because you're not engaging to the level you're capable of. What new weight—what heavier weight—do you need to reach for today?

Finally, we need to stretch.

Stretching in a spiritual sense could be *engaged rest* for our bodies and souls so that tensions don't build up too much in certain areas, limiting our range of motion—limiting our outreach and our love for others. Spiritually speaking, we need spiritual airflow; we need to breathe, we need good circulation, and we need deep breaths to best enjoy God and the life He's created for us to live. We don't want to get intensely strong and then get intensely injured because we didn't take care of ourselves. We don't want to be the strongest people in the ring—and yet tap out too early because we didn't make time to rest.

We talked about this already: Yes, this might literally be a nap. But that's not all it means. It doesn't just mean *disengagement*. It also means purposeful *engagement*. It also means engaged rest in the ways that bring your soul to life. Lengthen out. Stretch out. Steer into the skid of what brings you joy. Make those plans with friends, join that pottery class, go to that worship night, plan that getaway with your spouse, go one more night than you were going to, and make a plan for stretching in your life.

In the name of Jesus, refresh your rhythms. Refresh your relationships. Refresh your spiritual, emotional, and relational airflow. Reignite childhood wonder. Reengage with things that bring you joy. Pray and play in goblet, and try on new rhythms to see if they stretch your faith.

To keep going, you will need some sacred stretching.

Only carrying heavy weights all the time might sound noble, but the burden will hurt you. It's not admirable. Carrying too much leads to an inevitable, eventual defeat.

A Flourishing Vineyard

In the hills of Tuscany, amid the mountains of questions I had for sweet Niccolò, one question about longevity lingered on my lips. I had asked the secret to starting, and he gave me his two questions about soil and vision. I had asked about flourishing, and he confirmed I needed a trellis, needed to prune, and needed at times to freestyle. But now I wanted to know how to keep going. Is it adding on larger supports within the trellis each and every season? Would I be pruning more and more each year? Would I be harvesting the grapes, then immediately pruning the branches again?

So, I asked him, "After you begin producing the right kind of fruit, you have a harvest, right? What do you do after the harvest?"

He smiled and put his arms out, as if holding the world's largest plate.

"We make a big lunch! We celebrate!"

That was not what I was expecting.

I had figured that if trellises were so important to our flourishing, and pruning so important to our growth, then we must spend our lives pruning and building structures.

"Well, not every season can be that," he said. "The ground must also rest. And the people must also enjoy the harvest."

"I thought pruning was the most important."

"You can't just prune all the time," he continued. "If, after the harvest, you go back in and prune too early, the branches will grow too quickly and be more vulnerable to spring frost. It seems right at the moment, and if you're eager to get back to work, you might naturally want to do that—but it's not good for long-term growth. It hurts your next growing season."

When I got back to the States, I double-checked this with

my lab coat queen from Paso Robles, and she agreed. "Once the harvest is over, the vines begin to process by growing new roots. Now their goal is to absorb as many nutrients as possible. They need time to do that. The ground must rest, the roots must absorb. You can't just cut, cut, cut. You can't just produce, produce, produce. That's not good for the roots, branches, or fruit."

"It's not good for this year's harvest, right?"

"Oh, it's fine for this year's harvest," she clarified. "It's fine for this year's fruit. But we're not here for just *this year's* fruit. Our job is to make sure that what we plant is good for future years. Fifty-plus years' worth of healthy growth can happen if we do our part well today. If we know our soil, know our grapes, build the right trellis with the right supports, prune the branches, tend to the vine, water it, nurture it, harvest it, and then let it rest and absorb the nutrients it needs for the next season, the vine can produce far beyond our lives."

After following Jesus for most of my life, this is what I now know. Sometimes we think we have been called to produce, produce, and produce—to do more for God, to have greater impact, and to produce more fruit. But as we've unpacked, if we're not careful, we can produce lots of fruit that's *sour.* And not only that, we can exhaust ourselves and do damage to the Vine. We can hurt our souls, our families, our churches, and the reputation of God's church.

Or we can think that all we need to do is prune. All we need to do are the hardest things *we could possibly do.* All we need to do is sacrifice *more.* And if we are not careful, we can prune too much and cause damage when we should be nurturing the growth from the last pruning.

It might seem like constant pruning is good for our fruit today, but it's not good for our fruit tomorrow.

Instead, let's be aware of our seasons.

If you are not sure what season you're in, take time to ask God for direction and insight.

Maybe it's a season of studying your soil. *Or falling in love with your soil.*

Maybe it's a season of unearthing your vision.

Maybe it's a season of building or rebuilding a good trellis.

Maybe it's a season where you need to freestyle.

Maybe it's time to prune.

Maybe it's time to reap. Maybe it's harvest season. Maybe it's time to get into the dirt and witness the fruit of years of labor.

Maybe this is a season of rest and enjoyment. Maybe the ground needs to rest or the roots of your faith need to absorb nutrients. You aren't resting to avoid work or because you aren't good at tending the plant; you rest because you care about the quality of the fruit and the longevity of the flourishing vineyard.

Maybe you need to enjoy the harvest.

Or maybe it's time to start planting again . . .

I don't know where you are in your faith. But I know this is not a linear journey. You do not arrive at a specific place in your life and stop growing because your faith is done. Jesus did not call us lifeless pieces of deadwood. No, Jesus called us branches that are meant to continuously bear fruit in God's growing vineyard.

Maybe it's time to start planting again . . .

So—how can your relationship with God continue to flourish?

How can this stay real for you?

A life of rhythm and power, power and rhythm.

A life of prayerfully adding new weights and consistently stretching.

A life of purposefully paying attention to your fruit and coming to God—the Gardener, the Vinedresser—and asking Him to reveal the next way He is calling you to grow.

This way, you can do more than just produce fruit. You can have an ongoing, fruitful life.

CHAPTER 19

The Best Time

My husband is fifth in a generational line of farmers on the outskirts of Cherokee, Iowa. Our family farm is primarily a corn and soybean farm, and back in the day, it also had quite a bit of livestock. Up until my research on abiding, I didn't understand anything about farming. I grew up on the streets of San Francisco, so I know about how to freestyle and play poker and I'm an expert at thrift shopping. But there's quite a bit in the Bible about harvest, since agriculture was a common way of life to the people Jesus was talking to. Jesus specifically referred to the harvest as people who are in need of God, "deeply distraught, malaised, and heart-broken. They seemed to Him like lost sheep without a shepherd."[1] He called the great opportunity for people to know Him as "a huge harvest!"[2] Jesus, Niccolò, and my wine friend in her cool lab all talked about how "a harvest is coming."

But this sort of language was not common to me.

So I called my father-in-law, Papa Bill. (Yes, this is the four-hundredth story of me asking an expert on something I know nothing about. I'm very good at not knowing things.) I asked him, "Is harvest time easy or hard?"

I was not sure. I'd heard preachers who are not farmers talk about harvest in a variety of ways . . .

One preacher said it should be the easiest thing because as it relates to Scripture, we're *made* to do it. Because God says He's in charge of the harvest, the harvest should be easy. It should involve leaning back, kicking up our feet, and trusting God to do the work.

I get that.

Yet I'd heard another preacher say the harvest is the hardest part. You wake up early and you go to bed late. It's rough! "The corn isn't going to pick itself," he said. "It's time to get to work!" The point was that the harvest part is difficult, but it's worth it.

I get that too.

So I had heard two different perspectives, and I just didn't know the truth. But I figured a farmer would. Someone who has been a part of an actual harvest.

I explained all of this to my father-in-law and was expecting him to pick one of those two categories. I pressed, "Which is it? Is it the easiest time or the hardest time?"

And he chuckled.

"Well," he said, "it's the best time."

He continued, "It's fall. Everything is crisp and clear. And the smells are amazing and vibrant. Grain itself has a great smell. The weather is inviting. We all look forward to this moment. This is what we've been working for. This is the whole point."

"So it's easy?" I said.

He let out a loud laugh before he exclaimed, "No! It's intense! Oh, it's such hard work, and it's certainly not always pretty. It *does* take getting up early sometimes, and it does take patience, sweat, and resilience. If one person gets sick, other people from other farms come and help. It can be a lot of last-minute decisions, and we have to be flexible and on our toes and there's a lot you can't plan for."

He then paused, as if reminiscing about the days he worked in those conditions, recalling the truth of what they were like. "But," he said, "because of the atmosphere of a harvest, it doesn't *feel* too intense. We're all doing it together, excited together, working together. Yes, it's intense, but it's the best part. We didn't go through all this to miss enjoying the harvest. The work fails in comparison to the joy."

I gushed in my response. "Oh, my goodness. That was the most powerful thing I've ever heard about harvest!"

Surprised, he said, "It was? What did I say?"

I laughed. He was just telling me about his childhood, and I was having a full-out revival in a Courtyard by Marriott.

As someone who has been a part of sowing, watering, and reaping in the harvest of souls, I was starting to see what he was talking about.

I think back to growing up and serving at our outdoor, inner-city church two or three days a week until I was seventeen. I think about my friends living without homes and battling addiction, and I remember all the colorful memories that came with that kind of childhood. I think about packing the lunches, folding the clothes, setting up and taking down chairs, giving haircuts, praying for people, breaking up fights, helping people up from the floor, and cleaning up afterward, just to do it all again in a couple of days.

I think about the days of rain or immense heat when we set up tents and the times someone in my family or on our team was hit, pushed, assaulted, or spit on. I also think about the times people laid their bottles of alcohol on the "altar" (a brick ledge with graffiti all over it), along with heroin needles, crack pipes, knives, and other things they'd used as weapons. I think about seeing them kneel on hot (or wet) cement as they gave their lives to Jesus, knees drenched in sweat or rain.

I think about those who later started serving with us, or in other churches, and those who after they got their fresh haircuts and new clothes went on job interviews and started new lives. I think about a woman who once came with a documentary crew because she had given her life to Jesus at our outdoor church and was now the founder of a thriving ministry for under-resourced women to have a safe place for recovery and restoration. She came with her staff. She wanted to show them where her life had changed. She never imagined that the same preacher and the same family that were there eleven years before would still be there—still seeing lives like hers changed.

I've seen the harvest. And I can tell you: It's intense. It's hard. It's not for the fainthearted. And also, it's the best.

Today, through my lens of what I've seen of the global church—the ones with stained glass windows and choirs, the ones with loud music and bright lights, various outreaches around the world, and individuals sharing about Jesus—I can say it with even more certainty: It's still the best.

And we didn't go through all this—the sowing, the watering, the patience, the forgiveness, the service, the generosity, the stretching of our lives, and the trials we've overcome—to *not* reap the harvest.

This is Jesus' kind and wonderful invitation to us: Come to God with your background, personality, and unique details, and tell others they can come with all theirs too. Invite everyone you know into this freedom. Tell everyone you know that they also have permission to enjoy God in their unique way. Come be a part of the intense and the amazing, the awkward and the hard—the best thing you'll ever be invited to.

The Great Uncomplicating

One more thing I want to share before we end our time together. The last noodle I want to untangle. Right before I got off the phone with Papa Bill, I said, "Well, thanks for telling me what it takes to be a good farmer!"

And he said, "Well . . . to be clear, hun . . . to be a *good* farmer . . ."

Uh-oh.

"To be a good farmer, you actually have to be a good mechanic."

If there's anything I know *less* about than farming, it's mechanics.

"Say more."

"You get up early in the morning to make sure your mechanics are working properly," he said. "You might be up between five and seven a.m. getting ready for your day. Checking the mechanics on your tools, sharpening them, oiling them, checking the gears in your combine that you'll drive to take the cobs of corn off the plant. There's a bunch of different things. Because if the mechanics aren't tended to, if they're broken or faulty, then there's no way to be a good farmer, and it hurts the harvest."

He continued, "For example, you could go through the field on your combine, and something in the machinery is wrong, and something clunks, and now you're done. You're stuck. If you haven't been consistent in attending to your mechanics *before* the field, you won't do too well *on* the field. There are hours of preparation for your tools."

"So you're done? The harvest is over before you even start?"

He chuckled. "Oh, no. You just gotta fix what's been broken. You might need to go back and fix your tools, or you might need a more seasoned mechanic—someone who is better at keeping their tools—to help you so you can continue. That's all."

Thank you, Papa Bill.

Before we end our time together in these pages, I want to leave you with this:

Some of us may need to tend to our mechanics: our one-on-one relationships with God. And if we are unable to do that, we may need to open up to someone—a trusted friend or a pastor or a counselor—to show us how to better tend to our mechanics. This is why we must make it a point to practice closeness, to get real with a safe community.

We may have broken things within us. Those things can hurt us and hurt the harvest.

I can tell you that there was a time in my life years ago when I was publicly serving God while privately mad at God because of things taken from me, words spoken against me, unjust things that happened to me, and some regrets of my own. And it took me years to acknowledge what was broken within me. The ways I refused to surrender. The ways I refused to forgive. The ways I refused to truly and fully let God in and allow real healing to take place. As a result, I was not living the full and authentic life God created me for. I was not kind. I was not filled with peace. And I was not a living example of the love and grace that God gives.

The way to live out your God-given purpose, to flourish and enjoy the harvest, is to first have a one-on-one relationship with Jesus that is real, tended to, and cared for. The mission will be accomplished if the mechanics are prepared.

Jesus once said to His students, "The harvest is plentiful but the workers are few."[3]

Jesus was not saying the world isn't ready.

Jesus was saying the world is ready.

The church is not.

It's possible the harvest is plentiful but the workers are unprepared.

It's possible the harvest is plentiful but the workers are overcomplicating it.

It's possible the harvest is plentiful but the workers have mechanics to work on.

One reason why so many people outside the church are far from God is because so many people inside the church are far from God. We need a real relationship with Jesus ourselves *first.* We need to surrender our sin, our pride, and our egos and lay them at the feet of Jesus. Then we can know Jesus for real and show a watching world what He is actually like.

The mission will be accomplished if the mechanics are prepared.

What might be broken that needs to be repaired?

Some of us have lost our joy in following Jesus. Some of us don't make any time to talk to Him. Or when we do talk to Him, we're not real with Him. Some of us are too busy to follow Him. Some of us are overthinking the right way or the right time to follow Jesus. Some of us are following Him publicly while ignoring Him privately. Some of us don't want to heal. Some of us aren't remotely interested in sharing the love of Jesus. Some of us think the Great Commission—Jesus' final words and His central instruction to all His followers to share the gospel, make disciples, and build God's church—is a *good* commission for some but not for us.

But the harvest is ready.

I want you to know: You *are* called to share God's love with people all around you throughout your lifetime—in your real life, with your real personality. But make no mistake, the first and foremost important part of your calling is to know Jesus for real yourself. And if we are not participating in the harvest, then something is broken in the mechanics.

I hope this book is like an owner's manual for any parts of your relationship with Jesus that need to be tended to.

While Jesus walked on our earth, He called us the salt of the earth. He said, "Salt is good, but if salt has lost its taste, how can its saltiness be restored?"[4]

It's a good question.

Eugene Peterson writes in response, "The answer to his question is simple. It can't. You have to go back to the salt mines. You have to dig some fresh salt."[5]

There is a way to tend to what's broken within us.

Surrender your whole life to Jesus. Come before Him with all the honesty and grit and realness your soul can muster. Invite Him into the deep interiors and broken places. Do this again and again throughout your whole life.

As you hit roadblocks, head back to part 2 of this book, then pick and choose what you might need in that season. If you need to be reminded of the unique ways you've been created to encounter God right where you are, head back to the chapters on shortcuts (part 3). Continue to pray and play, and let love be the measure the entire way. Let go of what's holding you back, and invite Jesus into every messy, unpretty, and unpolished moment of your real life. Uncomplicate your relationship with God, and with all your heart and with all your soul, go back to the salt mines.

Dig some fresh salt.

If we want to complete the Great Commission, we must first have a Great Uncomplicating. Uncomplicating what a real relationship with Jesus looks like for ourselves and uncomplicating what a real relationship looks like for others as well. When we do

If we want to complete the Great Commission, we must first have a Great Uncomplicating.

that, a great harvest *will happen.* The harvest will be ready. And the workers will be too.

This can be real *for all of us.*

That is what I hope you've unlocked in this book. This beautiful, freeing, simple truth:

You have permission from God to encounter and enjoy Him in your own unique way.

And you have the glorious invitation to give others that same permission.

And I promise you: *It's the best.*

Noodles of Thank-Yous

Thank you to the over one thousand people who shared so much about their relationships with God with me. I will never take it for granted. It felt like being let in on the most sacred secrets. And it's transformed my life. From the birds to the gyms, to the "cellular and ecosystem processes," to the stories of loss, triumph, Paralympic training, coloring books, and choral Christmas music . . . know your stories will inspire many for years to come. Thank you.

Thank you to my husband, Guy, for once again saying yes with me to sharing more of our wonderfully wild, imperfect, and beautiful lives. Thanks for showing me how uncomplicated our faith can truly be. Being married to you is a gift. You've changed my life. Thanks for being my partner on mission for Jesus and His church forever.

A special thanks to my family and friends for allowing me to share so many of our personal stories in these pages. From the PowerPoint presentations to the Not Crushing It Club, to the stories of our family farm in Iowa . . . these black-and-white typed words are vibrantly more colorful because of the stories of my loved ones, and I am so thankful for you all. Thanks for being my team, my OGs, my ride-or-dies. Llamas for everybody.

A very special thanks to my little brother, Elijah, whose stories remain a constant thread woven through all my books. He grew sick during the writing of this book, and some of it was written in a hospital room beside him. Elijah, thanks for allowing me to share so much of our lives and our stories with the world. I love you, you're my hero, and I know you're a hero to many others too.

My immense gratitude to Niccolò and Annibale, my wise and gracious guides in the hills of Tuscany. Our time together has had a profound impact on my life, and I know it will continue to impact many. How many, you might ask? *Well, it depends . . .*

To Ryan, the supercool winemaker of dreams from Paso Robles, thank you for putting up with me and teaching me more than I ever could've imagined about real growth and real flourishing. Bill Nye has nothing on you.

My love and gratitude to Lana, Sean, Abe, Amy, Mark, Juby, Jason, Bianca, Izzy, Melissa, Megan, Emma, and Jacqui, who were my super team during this project, loving and nurturing these one thousand stories with me and all the creative ways we brought these conversations to life.

All my gratitude to my team at Hosanna Wong Ministries, Word on the Street, W Publishing, Thomas Nelson, and HarperCollins. Ryanne, my copilot and pillar, I love you. Thanks for saying yes to this one; I know it was no easy feat. Damon, my publisher of publishers and fellow basketball enthusiast, thanks for saying this idea wasn't too crazy. (*Crazy*, but not *too* crazy.) Lisa-Jo, my editor who fell in love with trellises and birds and all these tender stories with me, thank you for helping me untangle all the noodles. To my book agent, Jenni Burke, thank you for loving Tuscany first and making me fall in love with it too. And to Rachel, Jocelyn, Katherine, Caren, Allison, Meg, and the entire team who brought these words to life and helped me share them with many, thank you. Thank you to this wonderfully brave and bold team for loving this message from day one. This one was so much fun. I love our holy and helpful, colorful noodle book.

And to you, the one holding these pages. Thank you for continuing the conversation. May this book mark the start of many more stories that you will unearth as well. I don't see this book as an ode to the one thousand conversations I *once* had but rather as a beginning to a thousand conversations *and counting* . . . May we continue to dig up fresh salt, untangle lots of noodles, and learn more about our amazing God and each other through all the unique ways we enjoy Him. I bet there are more shortcuts than we know. Let's discover all the stories. Even the ones with birds.

Notes

Chapter 3: What Am I Made Of?

1. John 15:4 TLV.
2. John 15:4–5.
3. "Upgrade U," featuring Jay-Z, track 10 on Beyoncé, *B'Day*, Columbia Records, 2006.
4. John 10:10 AMPC.

Chapter 4: Roadblocks and Shortcuts

1. John 4:20.
2. John 4:23–24 MSG.
3. John 1:12.
4. John 14:6 NIV.
5. John 4:23–24 MSG.

Chapter 5: Busyness

1. Psalm 37:3 NIV.
2. Proverbs 22:6; Deuteronomy 6:6–7; Philippians 2:4; Hebrews 10:24–25.
3. John 13:34–35 MSG.
4. 2 Corinthians 12:9 NIV.

Chapter 6: Distractions

1. Luke 10:19; Matthew 28:18; Ephesians 3:20.

2. Luke 18:35–43.
3. Luke 19:1–9.
4. Matthew 14:13–14.
5. Matthew 14:23.
6. 1 Corinthians 7:35 MSG.
7. "Dopamine and Serotonin: Our Own Happy Chemicals," Nationwide Children's Hospital, February 28, 2023, https://www.nationwidechildrens.org/family-resources-education/700childrens/2023/02/dopamine-and-serotonin.
8. "Serotonin: The Natural Mood Booster," Harvard Health Publishing, accessed June 28, 2025, https://www.health.harvard.edu/mind-and-mood/serotonin-the-natural-mood-booster.
9. Sabrina Brennan, *Brain Gym: 40 Workouts to Boost Your Brain*, illus. by Andy Goodman, card deck (Orion Publishing Group, 2023).
10. Ephesians 5:15–16.

Chapter 7: Grief

1. James 4:8.
2. Psalm 46:1.

Chapter 8: Shame

1. Hebrews 9:22.
2. Romans 5:18 NLT.
3. 2 Corinthians 7:10.
4. 1 John 1:9 NIV.
5. James 5:16 MSG.
6. Curt Thompson, *The Soul of Shame: Retelling the Stories We Believe About Ourselves* (InterVarsity Press, 2015), 141.
7. Brené Brown, *The Gifts of Imperfection: Let Go of Who You Think You're Supposed to Be and Embrace Who You Are* (Hazelden, 2020), 53.
8. Brown, *The Gifts of Imperfection*, 55.
9. Romans 8:1 NLT.

Chapter 9: Silence

1. Dallas Willard, *Hearing God* (InterVarsity Press, 2024); Pete Greig, *How to Hear God* (Zondervan, 2022); "Priscilla Shirer: Expect to Hear God's Voice," by Going Beyond Ministries with Priscilla Shirer, YouTube, 44 min., 42 sec., https://www.youtube.com/watch?v=Fks_l16qJwg.
2. John 10:3–5.
3. John 10:27 NIV.
4. John 10:27.
5. Greig, *How to Hear God*, xv.
6. John 14:26.
7. "Priscilla Shirer: Expect to Hear God's Voice."
8. Genesis 28:12; Numbers 12:6; Judges 7; 1 Kings 3; Job 33:14–16; Isaiah 6; Joel 2:28–20; Matthew 1:20–21, 2:13–19; Acts 9:10–11.
9. 1 Samuel 19:20; 1 Corinthians 14:1, 29; Ephesians 4:11–12; 2 Peter 1:21.
10. Exodus 3:1–14; Judges 6:17–21, 36–40; Acts 2:22.
11. 1 Kings 19:12.
12. Proverbs 27:17; Luke 24:30–31; Acts 17:24–28; 1 Corinthians 10:25–26; Hebrews 10:24.

Chapter 10: Expectations

1. Matthew 5:48 NIV.
2. John 15:11 CSB.
3. John 15:11.
4. Matthew 5:43–48 NIV.
5. Matthew 22:36–40.
6. Larry Osborne, *A Contrarian's Guide to Knowing God* (Multnomah Books, 2007), 114–15.
7. Ephesians 2:8–9.

Chapter 11: Personality

1. Ephesians 2:10 AMP.

Chapter 12: Praise-o-nality

1. Matthew 4:18.
2. Matthew 26:36.
3. Matthew 6:26–34.
4. Exodus 35:30–35 MSG.
5. Matthew 26:39 NIV.
6. Luke 19:40 AMP.
7. Genesis 12:7–8, 13:18.
8. Exodus 20:24.
9. Acts 3:1.
10. Luke 4:16–21.
11. Mark 2:27.
12. Eugene Peterson, *On Living Well* (Waterbrook, 2021), 114.
13. Mark 1:35.
14. Mark 6:30–32.
15. Matthew 4:1–11.
16. Luke 2:46.
17. Luke 5, 10, 19, 22, 24.

Chapter 13: Personal Structure (Trellis)

1. John 15:4 TLV.
2. John 15:4 MSG.
3. John 15:4–5.
4. Matthew 4:19, 16:24; Mark 8:34; Luke 9:23; John 1:43.
5. Peterson, *On Living Well*, 7.
6. Watchman Nee, *Sit, Walk, Stand* (Tyndale, 1957), 27.

Chapter 14: Practical Supports (Rhythms)

1. Luke 6:12.
2. Mark 1:35.
3. John 6:11.
4. Matthew 26:36–39.
5. John 11:40–44.

6. Luke 22:32.
7. Luke 4:42; Mark 1:35.
8. Mark 6:31–32.
9. Mark 4:38 CEB.
10. Luke 2:41–52.
11. Genesis 4:4.
12. Genesis 22:3–5.
13. Logos Bible Study (Faithlife, 2024), https://www.logos.com/.
14. Romans 12:1.
15. Matthew 11:25 NIV.
16. Philippians 2:8 ESV.
17. Dallas Willard, *The Spirit of the Disciplines: Understanding How God Changes Lives* (HarperCollins, 1991), 180.
18. Peterson, *On Living Well*, 30.
19. Psalm 32:5 MSG.
20. 1 John 1:8–10 MSG.
21. Matthew 26:39 NLT.
22. James 5:16 MSG.
23. John 3:22 MSG.
24. John 3:22.
25. Luke 5:29–31.
26. Luke 7:36–50.
27. Matthew 11:18–19.
28. John Ortberg, *The Life You've Always Wanted* (Zondervan, 2002), 119.

Chapter 15: Play

1. Mark 1:35.
2. Luke 6:12, 22:39–41.
3. Matthew 14:23, John 11:41–42.
4. Peterson, *On Living Well*, 149–51.
5. Jeremiah 29:13 CSB.
6. Jeremiah 29:13–14 MSG.

Chapter 16: Prune

1. John 15:1–2 NIV.
2. J. Carl Laney, "The Vine, the Branches, and What It Means to Abide," in *Lexham Geographic Commentary on the Gospels*, eds. Barry J. Beitzel and Kristopher A. Lyle (Lexham Press, 2016), 435.
3. Laney, "What It Means to Abide," 435.
4. Laney, "What It Means to Abide," 435.
5. John 15:16 NIV.
6. John 15:16 AMP.
7. Psalm 139:23–24 NIV.
8. Psalm 139:23.

Chapter 17: How Do I Know If This Is Real for Me?

1. Martin Vincent, *Vincent's Word Studies of the New Testament* (Zondervan, 1997), 2:145.
2. Galatians 5:22–23 MSG.
3. Galatians 5:22–23.
4. Matthew 23:3 MSG.
5. Matthew 23:4 MSG.
6. Matthew 23:5–7 MSG.
7. Matthew 23:14.
8. Matthew 23:15 MSG.
9. Matthew 23:23–24 MSG.
10. Matthew 23:25–26.
11. John 13:35 NLT.
12. 1 Corinthians 13:1–3.
13. Adapted from 1 Corinthians 13:4–7.
14. 1 John 5:3.

Chapter 18: How Do I Make Sure This Lasts?

1. 2 Corinthians 13:5–6 MSG.
2. 2 Corinthians 13:7, 9.
3. 2 Corinthians 13:5 AMPC.

Chapter 19: The Best Time

1. Matthew 9:36.
2. Matthew 9:37 MSG.
3. Matthew 9:37.
4. Luke 14:34 NRSVUE.
5. Peterson, *On Living Well*, 9.

About the Author

Hosanna Wong is an international speaker, bestselling author, and spoken-word artist helping everyday people know Jesus for real. Widely known for her spoken-word piece "I Have A New Name," Hosanna shares in churches, conferences, prisons, and other events around the world, reaching across denominations, backgrounds, and cultures.

Born and raised in an urban ministry on the streets of San Francisco, Hosanna later packed her life into suitcases and traveled to churches and other ministries throughout the United States to share about Jesus through spoken-word poetry. During those years without a permanent home, she began speaking and creating resources to serve the local and global church.

Hosanna currently travels and speaks year-round and serves on teaching teams at churches throughout the United States. She and her husband, Guy, serve together in various ministries, equipping people with tools to share the gospel of Jesus in today's world. Hosanna is the bestselling author of *How (Not) to Save the World* and *You Are More Than You've Been Told*.

About the Author

Free Videos, Resources, and More!

Unlock additional free videos and resources from Hosanna for your small group, church, or personal journey!

www.hosannawong.com/uncomplicateit-resources

How can we talk about Jesus without being weird or pushy? With honesty and humor, Hosanna Wong uncovers what the Bible actually says about revealing God's love in our everyday lives, and gives practical tools to show us how. We are more equipped than we know.

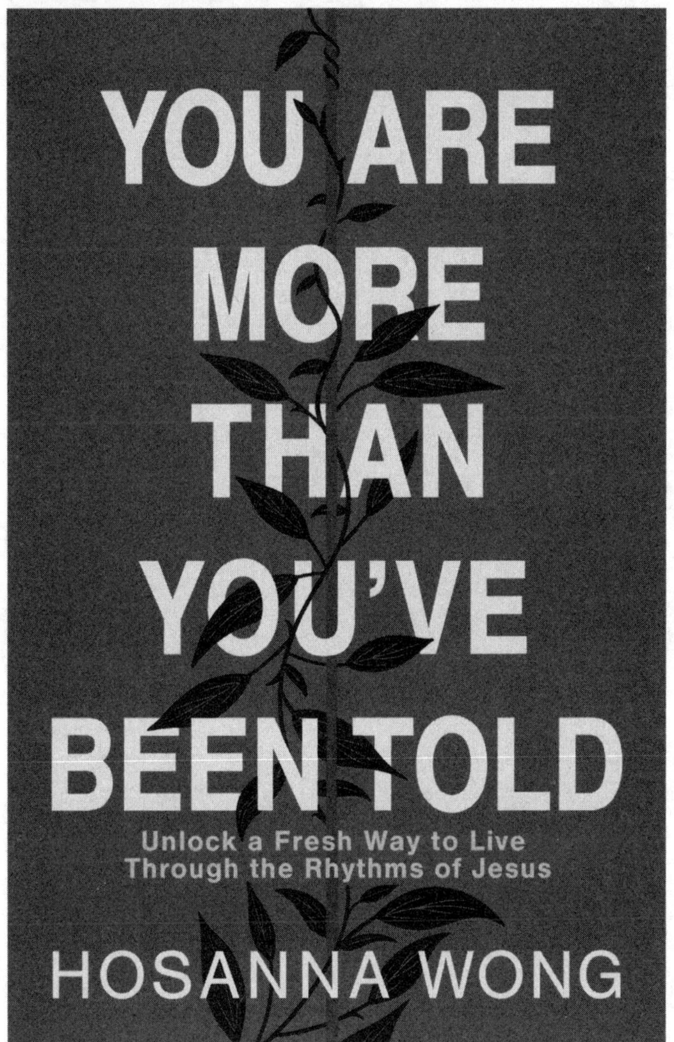

Have you ever felt unseen, unwanted, or unworthy? How can you know who you really are and how to live like it every single day? With tender vulnerability, Hosanna Wong asks the same questions and reveals how you are more than you've been told. You are more than what you've done or what's been done to you. You are what God says about you.